AN INNOCENT WORLD

by

DOUGLAS A. KING

An Innocent World

Second Edition

Copyright © 2020 by Douglas A. King

Tellwell Talent

www.tellwell.ca

ISBN

978-0-2288-2887-7 (Hardcover)

978-0-2288-2888-4 (Paperback)

978-0-2288-2886-0 (eBook)

DEDICATION

To Marion,
who taught me the importance
of logic when dealing
with people.

BOOK REVIEWS

A long-form thought experiment that presents a feast of fascinating existential questions, An Innocent World by Douglas A. King is an intriguing exploration of mortality and meaning. Thought-provoking for Christians, while simultaneously engaging for theologians, atheists, and agnostics alike, this unique read dissects common misconceptions about faith, offering a paradigm-shifting glimpse at another path for humanity.

This provocative thesis is founded on the premise that Adam and Eve already possessed immortality, rather than being tempted to eat from the Tree of the Knowledge of Good and Evil by its promise. King explores a variety of biblical contradictions, envisioning what a different origin point could have meant for human development and destiny, and whether the horrors and suffering we witness all around us could be avoided entirely.

King's thesis imagines a world with two distinct groups – the Innocents and the Guilty – categorized based on whether or not they had gained knowledge of good and evil by eating the fruit. Through this binary, the book asks readers to envision a different world, one without strife, guilt, and pain, and then play out the experience of daily existence, prompting us to consider which of those lives we would choose: blissful innocence without fear of death, or guilt-ridden struggle against the forces and consequences of evil.

A philosophical prize for radical thinkers and futurists, the book posits that imagining a better world is necessary before it can be created, a refreshingly different take than waiting for the future promise of heaven. There are exhaustive examinations of nebulous vocabulary, from "good" and "evil" to "knowledge," "benefit," and "sin," followed by the fascinating heart of the manuscript, which extrapolates the original Innocent vs Guilty conceit to the real world. Moving meticulously through different areas of modern life, from environmental crises and natural disasters to xenophobia, racism, wealth inequality, geopolitics, family structure, social support systems, media influence, and more, this fictional reality of an "Innocent" world comes into focus like a paradisical puzzle.

While the narrative elements occasionally rely on a leap of faith, King consistently employs logical reasoning to expand on his points. This rhetorical and logical diligence is the most impressive and eye-opening facet of the text, as it presents a close reading of Scripture and contemporary life through lexicological analysis, historical reflection, and mainstream understanding. The polished academic tone makes for a more approachable read, as the suppositions and arguments feel grounded in tangible ideas and clear contradictions, instead of feelings, beliefs, and dogmatic opinions.

That said, staunch atheists may still struggle to get past certain initial statements, namely that "all of us are here because we believe in God, even those that claim not to." There is a self-assurance to the writing that inspires reader investment and feels well-deserved, but could also be perceived to be overconfident, controversial, or even heretical. The author seems fully aware of this risk, but willing to take it for the sake of his broader argument, which is persuasive and in no way proselytizing.

Ultimately tackling the largest question that human beings face – why are we here and what purpose does existence serve? – this revolutionary proposal challenges both religious and secular readers to assess their personal belief structures and deepest sense of purpose, resulting in a mind-altering combination of religious writing, social science, and futurism.

-Self-Publishing Review

"An Innocent World" by Douglas A King, is an engrossing, thought-provoking "What if" Christian-based exploration of Adam and Eve. The author poses the question, "What would our world be like if Adam and Eve had NOT eaten the fruit of the Tree of the Knowledge of Good and Evil?" The answers that King arrived at comprise this intriguing work of non-fiction.

But there are more questions to consider and answer, such as, "Why was the Tree of Life, the Tree that gives immortal life, in the Garden of Eden, if Adam and Eve were already immortal?" Suppose that we earthlings could enjoy a carefree life rather than one destined to Biblical outcomes? These questions and answers may not be for everyone's palate, but if you read with an open mind, you'll find yourself perhaps wondering the same things.

King's logical approach to the questions and answers is unique and surprising, and it will cause readers to think outside the box, at least for a little while. Imagine our world is made up not of humans, but the traditional space alien, and that they are immortal- they'll live for eternity. If this is a world and way of life you can envision and hope for, you will enjoy this book and what the author has to say.

In King's world, this would be the way to strengthen character and naturally become closer to God. Those who choose the easy path would be called The Innocents, while the ones choosing the rockier path of building character, would be called The Guilty. This is an alternate view of the Bible-based narrative, showing what human history and earth would look like under that scenario, and one that is interesting to consider. This supposed existence may have you coming up with your own questions. I know I had mine: Would there be crime and violence in that different world? What would love and romance look like? Would there be a need for hospitals or doctors? How would this affect how we interact with one another? Some of my questions were answered in the book, but there are other topics, like sports, politics, and race.

I think books like King's can bring clarity to your own beliefs, not overthrow them, not jeopardize them. This book can serve to strengthen what you already believe, or maybe it can set you on a path toward changing the status quo here on earth and perhaps trying to make it a better place to live for everyone. There is a good balance of philosophy and reasoning, with some pop culture references--all combined in an appealing style. As you read, you'll feel like you're sitting in a really good philosophy class, listening to a really good philosophy teacher. For a book that makes you both think and feel, "An Innocent World" by Douglas A King, is a gem.

-Reviewed by Tammy Ruggles for
Reader Views (01/2024)

The substance of "An Innocent World" is fascinating. It's a nonfiction Christian book that puts forward the hypothesis that rather than being born into sin and thus automatically encountering pain and suffering during our lifetime as punishment, what if instead we were able to choose either a life of relative ease (and potential immortality) or a life of suffering and hardship in order to build character and grow closer to God?

The author suggests that those choosing the first path, the life of ease, could be called Innocents. They would be kind and compassionate, unable to intentionally cause harm. Thus there would be no crime, no war, no drug addiction, and no alcoholism. They would choose this path by eating the fruit from the Tree of Life (from the Garden of Eden), thus maintaining good health and longevity to the point of immortality.

Those choosing the second path, an arduous life of character-building in order to be closer to God when they die, would do so by choosing to eat from the Tree of the Knowledge of Good and Evil (choosing, rather than being tricked into it by a serpent). They are us, the Guilty, harming our planet and each other (and sometimes even ourselves) to the point of potential extinction and destruction of our planet through war, crime, selfishness, and greed.

-*Freelancer, Professional Critique and Review, Editor: Lee Ann Wolff*

PREFACE
SECOND EDITION

I had three goals in mind when producing this second edition of my book. One, that the logic be more consistent. In so doing, I had to move some chapters around. Of course, I had to strengthen some of the logic that already existed in those chapters to maintain a consistent flow. I also removed any inductive logic references and instead focused entirely on deductive reasoning. But with just those changes the book became more logical.

The second goal was to introduce more references. It was pointed out to me that I tended to make some statements, that to me seem obvious, but to others not so much. So, I added references to back up those statements.

Lastly, it was also pointed out to me that I should probably explain why I wrote this book in the first place, that it was not something just to fill my time, since I was now retired. My reason is explained in the Introduction.

I think that most everyone on this planet has, at one time or another, asked themselves why they are here. It's an important question that deserves an answer. In writing this book, it wasn't my intention to answer that question, but I did. However, I'll leave it up to you, the reader, to decide whether I have in fact done so.

TABLE OF CONTENTS

INTRODUCTION

Imagine you are being offered a choice as to which kind of life you can live. The first choice is an immortal life. In living this life you naturally behave in a caring and respectful manner towards your fellow humans, happy and content, never knowingly causing another harm. As a consequence, there is no crime and no war in your world. You can even worship God, if you like. Sounds like a good life, doesn't it?

However, there is another choice being presented to you. This one is a mortal life where you periodically experience suffering, sometimes great suffering, more than can be imagined. The purpose of this suffering is to give you the strength of character necessary to be able to meet Almighty God, face to Face. In doing so, you will be gifted with all the knowledge in the universe.

Which life would you choose?

———————————————

A choice of how to live is as important as life itself. However, according to the Bible, we're not given a choice, we are literally "born in sin".[1] What would our world be like if we were instead given a choice and decided not to be born that way?

For those of you unfamiliar with the phrase "born in sin", it's a summary translation from the Bible and means that we humans are born sinners, that sin is inherited, and that we have no choice in the matter. With condemnation like that, no wonder many people are turned off religion.

In this book, I use logic to answer the question as to what our world would be like. However, I use this logic with some religiosity.

In the process of answering that question, a number of conclusions were reached, some of which are: Being sinless does not guarantee immortality. Evil does not originate in us. We are not alone in the universe. We have lived past lives.

You might be asking why I chose to write this book, what inspired me to do it? It was dogs, specifically my working with dogs.

Subconsciously, I was looking for something that would explain the evil we live with every day in this world, why it seems so prevalent. I was yearning for something that did not hide evil behind the eyes.

My daughter has a dog walking/daycare business and I found myself working with her after I retired. In the process of working with dogs, I noticed they displayed a certain kind of behaviour that I had not been cognizant of my entire life. It was innocent behaviour, no evil intent. It was refreshing to see.

I never fully appreciated the statement "A dog is man's best friend" until I had a chance to work with them. They were always willing to accept love no matter what. They were overjoyed when their owners came to pick them up. When they did something wrong and you had to correct them, they always forgave you and never held a grudge. And when they wanted something, they were extremely polite about it. I couldn't believe there were individuals in this world that could behave that way. Wouldn't it be great if people were like that?

That's when I decided I had to write about innocence. What started out as a few pages became a book where I discovered truths about human nature that I wouldn't have believed possible. And I used a wonderful tool called logic to do so.

Most people seem to have a good understanding of what it means to be logical. But what is logic, really? Most of us, when we think about logic, think of just one kind: deductive logic. Deductive logic is truth-based, one truth following from a previous truth, so that the veracity of the final conclusion cannot be denied. In this book, I will use deductive logic exclusively.[2]

Sometimes in the logical process, it may not be obvious what the next step is. This is where intuition can play a role. You sense a hint of what the next step is, so you intuit it. This is the key to how I was able to get to where I have in this discourse: the reason for our existence on this planet. I also sense God's Hand in this process, so I don't credit myself entirely for any success I might have achieved.

In this book I will attempt to create a picture of a world inhabited by "Innocents", as I have termed them. Innocents are individuals who chose not to eat the fruit of the Tree of the Knowledge of Good and Evil as Adam and Eve did in the biblical Garden of Eden. Innocents are people without sin; they are incapable of evil thoughts. Moreover, Innocents can't tell the difference between good and evil.

Some of you may be thinking that a world made up of Innocents would be just an expanded version of the Garden of Eden, a kind of paradise. But after reading this book you will see that the world of the Innocent is not a paradise in the classical sense. It still had accidents, natural disasters, and even disease. The only thing it didn't have was human evil.

For those of you unfamiliar with the biblical story of Adam and Eve and the Garden of Eden, according to Judaism, they were the first people created by God. He placed them in the Garden of Eden to look after it and to populate the Earth.

Among the trees in the Garden there were two of special note: the Tree of Life and the Tree of the Knowledge of Good and Evil. God told Adam and Eve that they could eat the fruit of any tree in the Garden, including the Tree of Life, but they couldn't have the fruit from the Tree of the Knowledge of Good and Evil. If they did that they would die. However, Adam and Eve were tricked into eating the fruit of the Tree of the Knowledge of Good and Evil by Satan (disguised as a talking snake), and as a consequence, had sinned, were no longer immortal, were cursed by God, and were removed from the Garden of Eden. They were left to wander a harsh and diminished world, to make a life for themselves and their children, eventually through the generations culminating in the world we see today, the world of the Guilty. This story is known as "The Fall of Man."[3]

The story of the Garden of Eden has been around for at least 3,000 years, and depending on which position you take regarding Adam and Eve's immortality, the story presents a contradiction:[4] If Adam and Eve were sinless and immortal, why was the Tree of Life, the tree that gives immortal life, with them in the Garden? It wasn't needed, so why was it there?

There are those among you who believe that Adam and Eve were mortal while living in the Garden, and you wouldn't be wrong. Here, I begin with the premise that Adam and Eve were immortal while living in the Garden, but through logic,

I show that they had to have been mortal, but for reasons that may differ from your own.

This book is a record of the logical journey I have taken to address the implications that arose from solving the above biblical contradiction. At times I have backtracked, reiterated previous thoughts, and even reached interim conclusions that I later discarded. I've left those passages in to show that in thinking something through to its final conclusion, it is sometimes necessary to venture off the main path and travel down rabbit trails of logic to reach conclusions, before returning to the main path once more. Rest assured, it was all a necessary part of the logical process I had undertaken in arriving at the final conclusion: why we are all here.

In writing this book I discovered something about the two Trees in the Garden that I had not previously suspected: they play a central role in how one chooses to live. The one way is represented by the Tree of Life where one chooses an innocent, immortal life, a life that enables one to behave in a caring and respectful manner towards one's fellow humans, happy and content, never knowingly causing another harm.

The other way of living, this one represented by the Tree of the Knowledge of Good and Evil, brings a mortal life of guilt and suffering, sometimes great suffering, more than can be imagined. The sole purpose of this suffering is to enable us to build enough strength of character to finally be able to bask in the Magnificent but Terrible Glory of Almighty God.

From this path, one emerges a suffering hero, gifted with all the knowledge in the universe, finally able and worthy to stand before Almighty God.

Indeed, these are paths that we choose every day, to be innocent or guilty in our behaviour towards our fellow humans, to choose to be influenced by our guilty past or to ignore it and behave as we deem fit. Of these two paths, it is the tough one, the one with the suffering that is the correct one. Stay on that path, and you will eventually meet your Maker.

This book will show you that there is no other way to stand with Almighty God except by choosing the path represented by the Tree of the Knowledge of Good and Evil, with its consequent guilt and suffering. We, here on this planet, are currently on the correct path to Almighty God. This is why we are here. Indeed, all of us are here because we believe in God, even those that claim not to.

I've said "Almighty God" a number of times above in order to make a distinction between "God", the loving and benevolent god known to all that love Him, and "Almighty God", the Magnificent God of Raw Power and Might that would shake us to the core if we went into His Presence unprepared. This is the god that Moses and the Jews met on Mount Sinai.[5] And this is the god that we, on this planet, have decided we also want to meet.

IN THE BEGINNING...

What would the world be like if Adam and Eve had never eaten the fruit of the Tree of the Knowledge of Good and Evil in the Garden of Eden? Would we still have wars, terrorism, murder, rape, and the like? Would 9/11 have happened? Would we fear our fellow man? Would news be boring? Would the world appear differently from what we see today?

The implication we get from the Bible (Old Testament) is that being sinless means you will automatically be immortal. For example, when God warned Adam and Eve that if they ate from the Tree of the Knowledge of Good and Evil they would die, this implied that Adam and Eve were immortal.

Some would argue that what God meant was Adam and Eve would 'spiritually' die, not physically die. That may be true, but in this book I interpret the word "die" in its usual sense of physical death. Besides, if God meant that Adam and Eve would spiritually die, why didn't He just say so? Then we might not be arguing about what He actually meant, thousands of years later.

Another example is when Adam and Eve sinned - by eating the fruit of the Tree of the Knowledge of Good and Evil - succeeding generations lived shorter and shorter lives, implying that with the accumulation of sin, subsequent generations weren't able to live as long.[6] Extrapolate that backward and the implication is that being sinless means you will be immortal. In fact, the Bible (New Testament) went a step further by stating that "Adam sinned, and that sin brought death into the world", thus establishing explicitly the connection between being sinless and immortality.[7]

I was thinking about the Tree of Life in the Garden of Eden. It seems to me that its presence in the Garden represents a contradiction. Before Adam and Eve sinned they were immortal. That being so, why was the Tree of Life, the Tree that gives immortal life, with them in the Garden? When they sinned (ate from the Tree of Knowledge of Good and Evil), the Tree of Life became a threat, not only to Adam and Eve but to God as well. The threat to Adam and Eve was since they had sinned, they were no longer immortal, but by eating the fruit from the Tree of Life they would again be immortal, but then they would have to live forever with the consequences of sin (disease, disability, pain, heartache, etc.). The threat to God was that Adam and Eve would be like God, knowing the difference between good and evil and immortal, but potentially evil.[8] So, the Tree of Life in the Garden of Eden was, at best, superfluous and, at worst, a threat. So why was it there?

In order to answer that, we need to decide what kind of tree the Tree of Life is. Is it the kind that once you eat its fruit you become immortal in the sense that you can never die? Or is it the kind that grants you 'effective immortality' where you have to periodically eat its fruit in order to maintain your body indefinitely?

If it's the first kind (unconditional immortality), then once its fruit is eaten, we are back to the situation where the Tree of Life becomes superfluous and a threat.

So, it must be the second kind: a tree that maintains the body indefinitely. That being so, Adam and Eve would need to periodically eat the fruit of the Tree of Life in order to be effectively immortal. This means that the Tree of Life is a life sustainer, maintaining the body indefinitely, rather than a Tree that gives immortal life. Moreover, that maintenance must include the eradication of the body's diseases. Otherwise, there is no point in living forever, if you are chronically sick. Besides, it would be cruel and God would not permit that.

That is consistent with what the Bible says above. Subsequent generations lived shorter and shorter lives because they no longer had access to the Tree of Life to maintain their bodies. Whatever mechanism was maintaining the body – that had been periodically refreshed with the fruit from the Tree of Life - was slowly becoming less effective as the generations progressed.

I'm thinking that resisting the temptation to eat from the Tree of the Knowledge of Good and Evil was probably a relatively easy thing to do. If Adam and Eve had never known the effects of eating the fruit of the Tree of the Knowledge of Good and Evil, why would they be tempted to eat its fruit, especially if they were warned by God that it was deadly? The most they might feel is indifference, possibly some fear. As an example: if you had never tasted chocolate and someone in authority told you not to eat it, that it would kill you. Would you be tempted to eat it? Adam and Eve likely would have never eaten from the Tree of Knowledge if it hadn't been for Satan showing up. Without Satan, it was easy to "attain the mark set by God", in other words, to be sinless.

If it was so easy not to sin, why was Satan allowed to be in the Garden with Adam and Eve? Was it to make sin harder to resist? Why? Maybe it was to provide another dimension to the temptation to sin. A sinful object sitting there as a temptation provides its own persuasion, albeit a passive persuasion to sin. Perhaps God wanted to test Adam and Eve as to whether they could resist a more active persuasion to sin. That's where Satan comes in. Satan showed that Adam and Eve could not resist an active temptation to sin. Satan persuaded Eve to eat the fruit of the Tree of

Knowledge, claiming it would make her like God. She was tricked into eating it. She then persuaded Adam to eat the fruit as well. Thus, Adam and Eve were not fully resistant to sinning. But what if Adam and Eve had proved resistant? What was God's plan then?

That is the purpose of this book: to reveal God's Plan with regard to Adam and Eve choosing NOT to eat the fruit of the Tree of the Knowledge of Good and Evil, but instead choosing to eat from the Tree of Life.

I'm having second thoughts about my interpretation of the role of the Tree of the Knowledge of Good and Evil. For one thing, I have Adam and Eve being influenced by just the evil side of the Tree and not the good side. Later in the Bible, God acknowledges that Adam and Eve know the difference between good and evil, just as God does, and He was concerned that they would eat of the Tree of Life and be immortal like Himself. So God removed Adam and Eve from the Garden. There's something wrong with my interpretation of the role of the Tree of the Knowledge of Good and Evil.

Does the Tree of the Knowledge of Good and Evil represent a loss of innocence for Adam and Eve? What does it mean to lose your innocence? Does losing your innocence mean you have committed evil? Adam and Eve were innocent before they took the fruit of the Tree of Knowledge, but were they no longer innocent simply for having eaten its fruit? I would have to say yes because, for one thing, they had disobeyed God. And isn't that essentially what committing evil is, disobeying God? It wouldn't have mattered what the Tree of the Knowledge of Good and Evil was called; it could have been called Tree X, for that matter. It was that Adam and Eve had disobeyed God that made them no longer innocent. But what is interesting is that it was not their disobedience that got Adam and Eve thrown out of the Garden, but the threat they represented to God in that they might live forever, have knowledge of good and evil, but be potentially evil. So, Adam and Eve were no longer innocent on two counts: one, they disobeyed God, and two, they knew the difference between good and evil.

That leads me to another question: what does it mean to know the difference between good and evil? Does it mean you are aware of, have an understanding of, or have witnessed one or the other? Or does it mean you have experienced them?

The dictionary definition of the word "know" includes both understanding and experiencing. So the use of the word "Knowledge" in the title of the Tree of the Knowledge of Good and Evil must necessarily include those two concepts: understanding and experiencing. So, Adam and Eve, by eating the fruit, gained the understanding and the experience of the feeling of being good as well as the feeling of being evil.

God said that Adam and Eve would be like Him with their knowing good and evil and if they lived forever. That mutuality suggests God is not innocent. Thus, He must have experienced the feeling of being evil at some point.

I'm thinking about right and wrong, good and evil. Since they are principally terms that are defined by a society in order for its members to get along, they can have different meanings. For my purposes, I am going to restrict their meanings to something that I can use. Therefore, the term "right" will be restricted to mean the following: any action or omission that is beneficial to another, in terms of their survival. Whereas the term "wrong" will mean: any action or omission that is detrimental to another, also in terms of their survival. "Good" will then be defined as intending to do right, and "evil" will be defined as intending to do wrong.

The meanings of "beneficial" and "detrimental" are restricted to those actions or omissions that either enhance or diminish the survival of the affected individual. No other meanings are implied. I also do not make any moral judgments regarding the character of the recipient individual; I am only concerned as to how their survival is affected. So, a person, using my definition, would technically be right, although probably morally wrong, if they chose to benefit whom they consider to be an evil person, as long as they were enhancing the survival of that person. Conversely, they would technically be wrong, but probably morally right, if their action or omission diminished the survival of that evil person. I am not concerned with morality here, only survival.

Adam and Eve wanted to be able to discern between actions/omissions that are good from those that are evil. That seems reasonable to me, but apparently not to God. God wanted Adam and Eve to remain innocent, to not know the difference between good and evil. Though Adam and Eve were innocent before eating the fruit of the Tree of the Knowledge of Good and Evil and thus did not know the difference between good and evil, they were still capable of knowing the difference between right and wrong, the consequences of each being apparent from the point of view of coexisting within a society.

What do we really mean when we say that Adam and Eve didn't know the difference between good and evil? The only distinction I make in my definitions above is the idea of intention or feeling. I include the word "feeling" in my definitions because feeling like doing something is a form of intending to do it. So, when I say evil is intending to do wrong, I also include feeling like doing wrong in that definition. Likewise, when I say good is intending to do right, I also include feeling like doing right in that as well. Thus, when I say that Adam and Eve did not know the difference between good and evil, I mean they had no understanding of what it felt like to do either. To them, there was no difference because they had no feelings to distinguish one from the other.

Innocent is defined as doing nothing intentionally wrong. Conversely, the definition of guilty would be doing something intentionally wrong. As an innocent person, one could accidentally do something wrong and still remain innocent.

I think the point God was making was not to prevent Adam and Eve from committing wrongful acts - that would inevitably happen as time went on, even in their innocent state - but to avoid the situation where Adam and Eve felt like committing wrongful acts.

I'm sure Innocents would feel remorse if they accidentally hurt someone, but that's all they would feel. They would probably vow to avoid a similar situation that might result in a similar outcome, but they wouldn't feel guilty about it, since guilt is a word that has no meaning in the Innocent's world. Remember, you had to have committed evil (intentionally done something wrong, which doesn't happen in the Innocent's world) in order to have guilt. Another question: if an Innocent accidentally killed someone's loved one, would their relatives want revenge? Since they have no feelings of evil in them, these relatives might want justice, but they wouldn't want revenge, since revenge means intending to inflict harm on another, and is therefore evil, by definition. An eye for an eye, a tooth for a tooth, a death for a death, provided it is self-inflicted, is justice, but revenge tends to escalate the situation, making matters worse.

If we all lived in an Innocent world, would evil ever enter into it? Having the Tree of the Knowledge of Good and Evil in the Garden of Eden suggests that Adam and

Eve could have lived in a world without evil. It would have taken a deliberate act on their part, that is, eat from the Tree of Knowledge in order for evil to enter their world. Evil was not something that would have emerged as a statistical consequence of living in their world. So, no, evil would not be manifested in an Innocent world. Sure, there would have been accidents, natural disasters, but no evil acts.

This suggests another question: Are we basically bad or basically good? We are neither: we are basically innocent. Then where does evil come from? Does it come from our experience? No, it comes from the Tree of the Knowledge of Good and Evil. The evil we experience in our world does not originate in us, although we may facilitate it, it originates in the Tree of the Knowledge of Good and Evil.

How can I be sure of the truth of what I say in the paragraph above? When you think about the evil that we commit, it cannot stay with us when we die. If it did stay with us, we could not then choose to live an Innocent life. No, the evil we commit must originate from outside of us, only manifesting in the Guilty world and not beyond it.

What would the world look like if only Innocents lived in it? Certainly no crime, since crime is an act or omission that is intentionally detrimental to another. Therefore, there would be no robbery, no assault, sexual or otherwise, no murder, no terrorism, and no war. You wouldn't be afraid to go out at night since no one would want to hurt you. It would be a safe world.

INNOCENT OR GUILTY

Would the world of the Innocents experience natural disasters? Some people have suggested that in a world without sin, God would ensure no natural disasters would occur.[9] I think it needs to be realized that a world without sin is not Heaven, that the Earth will still undergo the same changes such as earthquakes, hurricanes, tornadoes, floods, etc. regardless of who inhabits the planet, Innocent or Guilty. Like a good parent, God wishes to build strong character in His children, whatever the circumstances.

In a sense, we the Guilty have more challenges, and thus more opportunities to build strong character than the Innocents. Innocents only have to deal with the aftermath of accidents and natural disasters, while we Guilty must also endure human evil as something to be faced and overcome. When all is said and done, the question that might be asked is: Who will have a more worthwhile character, the Innocent or the Guilty?

This question goes back to the Garden of Eden and the two Trees, the Tree of Life and the Tree of the Knowledge of Good and Evil, and why they were put there. Adam and Eve were presented with a choice: the Tree of Life and the innocence it represented or the Tree of the Knowledge of Good and Evil with its burden of guilt and pain. I'm beginning to think that both choices were equivalent in God's eyes. Choose one and you're guaranteed an Innocent, immortal life with fewer opportunities for building strong character but with more happiness and contentment. Choose the other and you inherit a Guilty, mortal life, which offers more opportunities for strong character building, but in the process you must face and overcome human evil. However, when you finally come out of it you will be a truly wise and worthy individual. It wouldn't be as large a crop, but it would be a better crop, if I may use an agricultural analogy. This also leaves us with the unsettling realization that possibly not all of us will make it. All this time, could we have been wrong about God's intent behind the two Trees in the Garden?

In terms of strong character building and the wisdom that comes with it, there is not a lot of opportunity to build a truly wise individual in the world of the Innocent. We are missing half the experience of living. In order to be a fully rounded, ultimately wise being, we would need to embrace the other half, the half that includes feelings of evil as well as good. It is not an easy choice. It requires deep commitment, great fortitude, and a willingness to plumb the depths of courage that most of us lack.

Imagine you're a parent and your child goes missing. You travel the same path your child did, asking people along the way, "Have you seen my child?" You frantically call everyone you know to find out if they have seen him/her. Finally, you are forced to call the police, realizing that your own efforts can't get your child back. If it's a small child, the police will probably get involved right away; otherwise, you may have to wait an agonizing 24 hours or more before the police begin to act.

Maybe you will be lucky and your child is found safe and sound. Then again, maybe you're not, and your child is either never found or s/he is found dead somewhere. Either way is torment, something I would not wish on my worst enemy. Not having lost a child myself, I can't imagine what it must be like to lose your own. It must be horrible, surely the worst kind of emotional pain one can endure. I can imagine nothing worse.

If you do manage to get your life together after losing your child under whatever circumstances, you deserve a medal. Even the bravest soldiers in war cannot boast of such courage. But how do you truly get over it? Do you try to forget it, in alcohol, drugs, how? There is no manual, no roadmap to show you the path to recovery. It's something that is unique to you. They're your memories, no one else's, and only you can choose how you are going to get on with your life. You might even choose to end your life because it's become too hard to bear after the loss of your child. Again, that is your choice. I wouldn't presume to tell you what you should do; you have to make that decision yourself. Whatever you decide, your time in this world of the Guilty may not be over. You could very well find yourself back here, in another life, ready or not to face its trials and tribulations once more.

Why would anyone in their right mind choose to live a life that includes the possibility of losing their child? Character building be damned. It's not worth it, the suffering, the pain, the loss. Who would be willing go through that? What is the upside that would make a person choose to suffer that way? I think that nothing short of being in God's Presence would make me willing to go through the suffering of losing my child. I presume that the rest of us feel the same way, otherwise you wouldn't be here. This has to mean that we know, as spiritual beings, what it's like to be in God's Presence. We must have been there at some point in order to know what we are missing. Next question: Why are we not still there?

God is Magnificent, but so Utterly Powerful, that we mere beings cannot take but a moment of His Terrible Presence. We thrill to be near but at such a cost that we cringe at the prospect of going naked into His Awesome Presence again.

We have to be prepared, build ourselves up so that we can at least appear worthy. But how does one accomplish that? There is only one way: to be like Him, to be comparable, to be kind of magnificent ourselves. That seems like a lot of work, the kind of work only a special few could do. Are we all willing to take the plunge and take on the suffering that God Himself, not to mention, Jesus, must have in order to become the Incredible Being that He is?[10] That requires only one road, and that is the road the Tree of the Knowledge of Good and Evil grows on.

What a god! To conceive of such a plan: use evil to do good, i.e. to facilitate our suffering in order to be with Him. A plan with all its intricacies and counter-intentions, with billions of lives to account for, all for the sake of reaping a relatively small harvest of supremely valiant, courageous, stalwart, incredibly wise and worthy individuals. And to do who knows what? It boggles the mind.

This notion of building strength of character through suffering in order to be close to God is not new, it's an idea that is mentioned in the Bible. Many scriptures speak of trials and tribulations in order to be purified enough to be with God. This is nothing more that character building through faith. I refer to the following scriptures: (all scriptures below are taken from the Word In Life Bible, Contemporary English Version)

James 1:12 God will bless you, if you don't give up when your faith is being tested. He will reward you with a glorious life, just as he rewards everyone who loves him.

Roman 5:3-4 But that's not all! We gladly suffer, because we know that suffering helps us to endure. And endurance builds character, which gives us a hope.

James 1:2-4 My friends, be glad, even if you have a lot of trouble. You know you learn to endure by having your faith tested. But you must learn to endure everything, so you will be completely mature and not lacking in anything.

Isaiah 48:10 I tested you in hard times just as silver is refined in a heated furnace.

James 1:3 You know you learn to endure by having your faith tested.

Matthew 7:14 But the gate to life is very narrow. The road that leads there is so hard to follow that only a few people find it.

Job 23:10 But he knows what I am doing, and when he tests me, I will be pure as gold.

1 Peter 1:6-7 On that day you will be glad, even if you have to go through many hard trials for a while. Your faith will be like gold that has been tested in a fire. And these trials will prove that your faith is worth much more than gold that can be destroyed. They will show that you will be given praise and honor and glory when Jesus Christ returns.

Zechariah 13:9 Then I will purify them and put them to the test, just as gold and silver are purified and tested.

They will pray in my name, and I will answer them. I will say, "You are my people," and they will reply, "You, Lord, are our God!"

These are just some of the scriptures that refer to the character-building testing of faith that God offers. For a more extensive list refer to the References section of this book.[11]

Faith helps you to endure suffering, to build the strength of character necessary to be with God and the Son of God, Jesus Christ.

We must, as individuals, be given a choice every time we're required to make a decision. If we find ourselves in the world of the Guilty, does that mean we chose this path, or was it chosen for us? In reading the story of Adam and Eve in the Garden of Eden, it seems like the choice is made for us, that we, the subsequent born, had no say in the matter. That can't be right. If anything, God believes in our power to choose. The Genesis account as written doesn't appear to give us a choice, that we're stuck with the bad decision Adam and Eve made in eating the fruit of the Tree of the Knowledge of Good and Evil. It appears that if we want life, then we must join the ranks of the Guilty. That doesn't seem fair, and I don't believe it's God's way of doing things.

No, I have to believe that if we want life, then God will give us the choice of which kind of life we want to live. Since there appears to be only two choices here: the Tree of Life or the Tree of the Knowledge of Good and Evil, and we happen to choose the Tree of Life, then where do we go to live? Obviously, we can't come here to the world of the Guilty. We must go to some other world, a world inhabited by fellow Innocents. I never did believe that we were alone in the universe. It seemed like such a terrible waste of space.

This notion of a populated universe - being supported by the freedom of choice God offers - suggests that the universe is populated by Innocent and Guilty beings, and no one else.

If I sound a little flaky here, so be it. I'd rather tell it like I see it than pretend I don't see it. The idea that we are not alone in the universe has been the logical outcome of the power of choice, as it was presented. I did not try to avoid the notion of a populated universe because it was uncomfortable to some people. I simply carried the power of choice to its logical conclusion, given the facts as presented in the story of the Garden of Eden. Some may view this story as mere fiction. I view it as highly symbolic in that events didn't transpire exactly as written.

What if I chose to eat from the Tree of the Knowledge of Good and Evil, but when I arrive I decide that, for whatever reason, I no longer want this life of guilt and pain?

You have two options: one, you can persevere and live out your life where, at the end of which, you will be presented with a choice to live a life of an Innocent. Or two, you can commit suicide. The first choice is the preferred one since it will provide you with opportunities to build your character, and in so doing, grow closer to God. The second choice, however, although quicker, will cause you to move further away from God since you are harming yourself. There is something else to consider: the path you are currently on may be the only correct one for you to finally meet God. Choose another path (by committing suicide) and it could end up destroying you.

I have subtly introduced the idea that we have lived past lives. I am aware that there are those who don't believe in that, that we have only one life to live. But look at it this way: Is God going to give us only one chance to be with Him, if we choose the Tree of the Knowledge of Good and Evil? It doesn't seem fair that Innocents get to live indefinitely in happiness and contentment while we Guilty are relegated to about 100 years of suffering, where we might not get to be with God as we had hoped. I have stated previously that God views the choice between the Tree of Life and the Tree of the Knowledge of Good and Evil as equivalent. I've also said that God is fair, and therefore would not present a choice that is so lopsided. If you had to make the choice under these conditions, which Tree would you choose? No, I have to believe that we are given multiple opportunities to be with God. Otherwise, I don't think I would want to participate.

Though we live in the world of the Guilty we can choose to not live that way. We can deny our heritage and decide that this life is ours alone, and nothing, past or present, has claim to it. None of the past evils that are possibly embedded in our DNA have a right to influence the proper living of our lives today. We can choose to be like the Innocent, to live our lives with integrity, to behave as if we had no evil in us, to simply choose to do no harm to another.

That seems like good advice, doesn't it? "Do no harm to another." Words to live by. But the world is a complex place and words like that won't necessarily get you through life unscathed. You will feel better about yourself, to be sure, but what ultimate benefit will it have in terms of your living in this world of the Guilty? Will your suffering be any less? Remember the parent with the lost child. If s/he had been living their life following the mantra "Do no harm to another," would the fact of their missing child cause them any less pain? I doubt it. Indeed, it might even make it worse. "Why has this happened to me? I've done no one any harm. I'm a good person. It's so unfair."

"God, where are you for me? Why don't You show up and relieve my suffering by returning my child to me? If only I hadn't chosen the Tree of the Knowledge of Good and Evil when I entered this life, then my child would probably be with me. They certainly wouldn't be in the hands of some depraved pervert doing who knows what to them."

Unfortunately, we did make the choice to live the life of the Guilty. We chose the hard path, the path with the possibility of incredible suffering. And we chose this path in order to be with God. Look at it this way: the greater the suffering you can take in this life, the closer you will be to God in the next. It doesn't make sense otherwise.

I would now like to justify my assumption that Innocents would not harm each other. Some may argue that my assumption is not supported by logic, but I can show that it is indeed logical. To illustrate, let's consider the opposite view: suppose Innocents were willing to harm each other. Accidentally, sure, but intentionally, no, since that, by definition, would be evil, something of which the Innocents would be incapable. Therefore, Innocents would be unable to deliberately harm each other.

THE TEN COMMANDMENTS

Would the Innocents require the Ten Commandments to govern their behaviour? The following is a listing of the Ten Commandments:[12]

1. Do not worship any other gods but Me
2. Do not make and worship idols
3. Do not misuse my name
4. Remember the Sabbath; do not work that day
5. Respect your father and mother
6. Do not murder
7. Be faithful in marriage
8. Do not steal
9. Do not lie about others
10. Do not want anything that belongs to someone else.

If the Innocents require the Ten Commandments to govern themselves, then evil has already entered their world.

One only needs to examine the sixth commandment, "Do not murder", to realize that adherence to this commandment means murderous thoughts must exist in the minds of Innocents in order for this commandment to become necessary. Since there are no evil thoughts in the minds of the Innocents, this commandment, at least, is not necessary.

Taking the trouble to create the Ten Commandments implies there is misbehaviour that needs correcting. Since disobeying God is considered evil, there would be no misbehaviour to correct among the Innocents. Therefore, none of the Ten Commandments are needed to govern the lives of the Innocents.

We've already seen that it would take a deliberate act like eating the fruit of the Tree of the Knowledge of Good and Evil for evil to enter the world. Evil is not a thing of substance but a thought, a feeling. Innocents could not be evil because they couldn't imagine what that's like. Otherwise, the existence of the Tree of the Knowledge of Good and Evil would have been unnecessary. Evil is a thought or feeling that would be completely foreign to the Innocents.

That Innocents would not need the Ten Commandments to govern their lives, suggests another question: Would Innocents have more than one religion? Examining the first Commandment "Do not worship any other gods but Me", we realize that if the Innocents didn't require this commandment, then they already worship only one god,

God. It's either that or they don't worship a god at all. Strictly speaking, they would not be disobeying this commandment, were that the case.

Could an Innocent get jealous? Jealousy is the flip side of the Envy coin. Envy is wanting what someone else has, which is strictly prohibited by the last commandment of the Ten Commandments, i.e. "Do not want anything that belongs to someone else." Since Innocents wouldn't require this commandment, envy is something they wouldn't have issues with. Jealousy is the converse of envy by not wanting someone else to have what you have. Jealousy and envy are different sides of the same equation. These are feelings that would be foreign to an Innocent.

In the following chapters, I will compare different facets of our world, the world of the Guilty, with those of the world of the Innocent. These facets will comprise various subjects ranging from "Agriculture" to "Appearance and Personality". I hope to produce a montage that, when taken together, will present a picture of what the world of the Innocents would be like.

This comparison is meant to illustrate the significance of which choice you make in answering the question "Which life would you choose?" first posed in the Introduction to this book. Your choice has the potential of creating one of two worlds: the World of the Innocent or the World of the Guilty.

AGRICULTURE

Agriculture: the basis of our food supply. Agriculture is not only about supplying food but other products as well. Products like biofuels, fiber, and medicine. Many of us think of land farming when we think of agriculture, but aquaculture, which is a category of animal husbandry, is also included under the Agriculture heading. Aquaculture produces fish, crustaceans, molluscs, aquatic plants, and algae for human consumption. Animal husbandry sources food from cattle, pigs, sheep, goats, chickens, ducks, and even horses, but can include any domesticated farm animal, llamas, for example. One third of the world's labour force is employed directly or indirectly in the agricultural sector.[13]

With all this enterprise involved in the production of food for our planet you would think we would have plenty of it to go around, certainly enough to feed the over 8 billion who live here. The answer is that we have the potential to feed everyone, especially since the Green Revolution which began in the

1930s that saw higher yields in cereals, wheat, and rice through the use of chemical fertilizers and agro-chemicals such as pesticides and herbicides and a controlled water supply. Most of the success of the Green Revolution has occurred in developing countries: Mexico, Brazil, and India, are examples.[14]

So why is about 10% of the world's population going hungry?[15] One reason is the energy crisis and dwindling petroleum sources. This has caused governments to develop alternate energy sources, among them the growing of biofuels, which are derived from the fermentation of corn or sugarcane, for example. This has squeezed out land normally used for food production. It is estimated that between 2.5 and 3.8% of arable land will be turned over to the production of biofuels by 2030.[16]

Another reason that so many of us go hungry is not everyone can afford to buy the food they need. A crop failure or two can switch a country from an exporter of food to an importer, and if that country is already poor, many of the people won't be able to purchase the food necessary to properly sustain themselves. The unaffordability of food is not just a Third World problem, we are experiencing it here in North America as well. Many of the poor can't afford to eat nutritionally because of high food prices.[17] And with projected increases in the amount of biofuel production that will replace food production coupled with an ever growing population, the situation will likely get worse.

Fortunately, progress is being made on at least one front to mitigate this issue of world hunger. It is an effort to convert deserts into arable land, and not how you might think. Deserts do get rain, just not very often. And since deserts are primarily found in the hotter climates, any rain that does fall is rapidly evaporated. A new product has been developed called Hydrogel Film, a superabsorbent polymer that can retain up to 1,000 times its weight in water. It is either spread out on a surface that can catch the rain or mixed into the desert soil. It is nontoxic and allows water and dissolved nutrients to feed the growing plant.[18]

What about genetically modified organisms such as plants and seeds? Success of GMOs has been mixed. Some countries either restrict the sale of foods affected by gene-splicing biotechnology or ban them altogether. There are benefits for farmers that use GMOs. They don't have to use conventional pesticides and herbicides with their detrimental effects on the environment. They also don't have to till their fields, which releases toxins in the form of leftover fertilizers, pesticides, and herbicides that lie in the ground.[19]

Monsanto, a leading advocate for GMOs recently ran a test of its Roundup Ready® Soybean, a plant that had been genetically modified to be resistant to Roundup, a broad spectrum herbicide. The original experiment ran fine in the lab. Weeds were killed and crops weren't. However, out in the real world, the result of the experiment was the creation of a so-called superweed. The problem is there just isn't enough genetic diversity with the relatively few varieties of weeds found in the laboratory plots to reveal those that can resist Roundup. In the real world of millions of acres and thousands of varieties of weeds, some were found that could resist the Roundup herbicide. These superweeds, of course, bred and spread throughout the land. To get rid of these superweeds, multiple and varied applications of conventional herbicides were necessary, which rather defeated the purpose of using GMOs in the first place.[20]

Approximately 10% of the Earth's surface is arable, capable of producing crops for consumption.[21] This is in keeping with the notion that the Guilty world should be a harsh and diminished place to live for its occupants; these conditions aiding in character development.

In contrast, virtually all the land on Earth would be arable for the Innocents. If we include the food sourced from the world's ocean's, this translates into an almost inexhaustible supply of food for the Innocents.

Distributing food would not be problem either with so much arable land about. Distribution networks would tend to be short and quick. This is unlike in our world where whole countries face starvation: Nigeria, Yemen, South Sudan, and Somalia, are examples.[22] Aid that is sent to them is sometimes stolen by corrupt officials who are supposed to be helping their people.[23] Unfortunately, it shows the depth of evil that humans are capable of facilitating, to be able to stand by and watch as their neighbour starves to death. It's enough to make you weep.

Would there be starvation in the Innocent's world? Since starvation is detrimental to humans, Innocents would see to it that starvation does not occur, if it can be helped. Crop failures happen, so people will go hungry. But starvation is something that takes a while, enough time to forestall it from happening. Allowing it to happen would let evil enter the world, which is something Innocents would be incapable of doing.

Would there be impoverished regions in the Innocent's world similar to ours? There probably would be an imbalance in the development of the various regions of the Innocent's world. Some would be more successfully developed than others. However, developing one region of the globe at the expense of another would not be tolerated, since that could bring harm to other Innocents. Innocents would view any imbalance honestly and without prejudice.

That is unlike in our world where the North American Free Trade Agreement (NAFTA) between the United States and Mexico has caused an increase in the migration of Mexican farm workers to the U.S. looking for work because they can't get a decent price for their produce at home. The reason for this disparity in produce prices is because the U.S.

subsidizes its own producers while Mexico does not. This imbalance has existed since before the NAFTA agreement was forged about two decades ago and, as of yet, no attempt has been made to rectify this situation.[24]

ENVIRONMENT

Our environment consists of air, water, land, animals, and plants. If we knowingly engage in a polluting activity which negatively impacts others then that constitutes intent, and therefore is considered evil, by definition. No matter how remote the possibility, if we deliberately send pollutants into the environment which can harm another person directly or indirectly, then we are guilty.

We, the Guilty, have been negligent in our responsibilities towards this planet. The way things stand right now, we have major pockets of pollution in the world. Air pollution exists in many cities and regions around the world. Some cities in Nigeria, Pakistan, and Iran are very polluted.[25] Hong Kong in the Peoples Republic of China has air pollution so severe at times that outbreaks of asthma and bronchitis are common.[26] Though not from air pollution, the most polluted city in the world is Chernobyl in the Ukraine, site of the worst nuclear power plant disaster in history.

The Chernobyl nuclear plant meltdown in 1986 was so severe that over 233,000 square kilometres were irradiated. Easterly winds spread the radioactivity throughout much of the northern hemisphere that included Europe, England, Ireland, Scotland, and Wales. Planes were grounded and venturing outside was discouraged. And now with Russia's recent armed takeover of this plant as well as the Zaporizhzhia plant, the threat of another nuclear disaster is renewed. [27]

Though 30 people died as a direct result of the Chernobyl explosion, it is difficult to put a number on indirect mortalities due to the unreliable data that was provided from the site and the different approaches at that time to quantifying the projected mortality. Even today, 35 years later, Chernobyl is a restricted area, with people not allowed to live there. Of course, some people will take a chance because they have no choice.[28]

The Chernobyl nuclear plant disaster was the direct result of man's hubris and negligence. However, another nuclear plant disaster resulted from Nature's fury. This time at the Fukushima Daiichi plant in Japan in 2011. It was brought down by a tsunami that resulted from a seaquake.

Miraculously, there were no fatalities at the Fukushima Daiichi site, but up to 1100 radiation-related deaths are estimated in the decades to come. The plant is expected to be out of service for 30 to 40 years, at which point it will be dismantled.[29] In the meantime, it serves as a reminder that we cannot guarantee the safety of our nuclear plants. Nature will sometimes have its say. Would Innocents build nuclear plants? They might, but only if they could guarantee their safety and the effective neutralization of nuclear waste.

Water pollution, in many ways, can be as much of a threat to human health as air pollution or nuclear plant disasters, since many cities and towns use their polluted rivers as a necessary source for their water, for drinking, bathing, and cooking. Unfortunately, many residents that deal with water pollution day to day eventually tolerate it, taking few precautions, considering it a necessary evil.

Currently there is a list of 12 of the worst polluted river systems in the world, and if you think that water pollution is a Third World problem, think again. The United States has two of the most polluted rivers in the world: the Cuyahoga River in Cleveland, and the Mississippi River, which spans several states.[30]

Not to be outdone by the U.S., two rivers that are even more polluted are located in India (the Ganges) and Indonesia (the Citarum). The Citarum River is rated the most polluted, with pollution so thick that the residents can't even see the water. The main source of pollutants is industrial waste from factories located along the river.[31]

What would be the state of our planet's environment if the Innocents were in charge? Certainly no polluted waterways, air pollution, or nuclear plant disasters. With the Innocent's inherent desire not to bring harm to another, this would translate into a clean environment in which fellow Innocents can live and thrive.

We, the Guilty, don't seem to have the wherewithal or the motivation to protect our workers and the environment when it is really needed. Here in the developed world, business does take a more responsible role in protecting the environment and their workers, mainly because it's the law. However, it was not always so. One only has to look to the developing world to see what it probably was like for the worker and the environment in the early stages of our own development.[32] It's sad that the All Mighty Dollar should have ruled our business community to such an extent that the protection of our workers and the environment came second.

Any activity involving the environment has the potential to pollute, so I don't see how Innocents, with their own industrialized society, would be able to avoid polluting their environment to some degree. Of course, Innocents would not intentionally pollute their environment. But what about unintentionally?

The environment is something we all share, such that any negative impact on it could affect us all. Innocents would make a special effort to maintain a healthy environment for the sake of fellow Innocents. Undoubtedly, any accidental environmental damage would be cleaned up right away. However, situations may arise where pollution is not immediately apparent and may go unnoticed for some time before being dealt with. But dealt with they will be. And in the safest and most expeditious way possible so as not to prolong the damaging effect on the environment.

RACE, SKIN COLOUR, LANGUAGE, AND BORDERS

Would there be different races, skin colours, or languages in the Innocent's world? Would there be borders? That there are different races and skin colours is primarily because people live in different regions of the planet. Certain environmental conditions have given rise to different skin colours. For example, more exposure to intense sunlight, either directly or indirectly (reflected light from snowpack), will cause the skin to darken. This is because exposure to ultraviolet light causes the skin to darken over time due to the presence of melanin in the skin. Melanin is a brown pigment that reacts to UV radiation to darken the skin as a means of protection. The more intense UV radiation in the equatorial regions translates into darker skin. The levels of ultraviolet radiation reaching the polar ice caps are almost doubled with its reflection off the snow, thus contributing to the darkening of the inhabitants there. The temperate regions receive less UV radiation and as a consequence have less darkening of the skin. Skin colour is closely associated with race and is how we generally identify one from another.[33]

Why do we have different languages? There are many theories but very little agreement. Even the Bible has its own idea: the different languages were the result of God confounding the speech of the Babylonians when they attempted to build a tower to Heaven.[34] With so much disagreement on the subject, I'm motivated to submit my own theory to the debate:

About 60,000 years ago, native Africans began migrating out of the continent into every other part of the world, including the Americas.[35] With the invention of agriculture, people settled down into pockets of civilization. If I can use Charles Darwin's observations of the finch species that inhabited the Galapagos Islands, I will attempt to establish a logical similarity between the mutation of island species that are kept in isolation from their mother species on the continent and the 'mutation' of languages among people who find themselves cut off from their cousins.

Species in isolation, such as on islands, tend to change their behaviour and appearance more rapidly relative to those on the continent for two reasons: one, as a behavioural adaptation in order to become more suited to the new environment as a means of survival, and two, because their gene pool is smaller and thus containing fewer mitigating choices, changes in appearance of the isolated species would tend to be more dramatic. These influences would result in a more noticeable difference in behaviour and appearance between the island and the continental members of the same species.[36]

Extend that idea to languages. Let's view the original language as the mother tongue of the various languages that developed in the relative isolation of the agricultural communities that started to appear about 12,000 years ago.[37] Each community left on its own would tend to develop language variants, i.e. dialects, since they no longer have access to the general population and the mother tongue to keep them in line linguistically. Over time, these variants would become more pronounced as they forget more and more of the mother tongue due to lack of use, mainly because of their more specialized agricultural activities and its associated vocabulary. As they reduce their 'genetic pool' of words, other words may be created and substituted when needed. Given enough time, their language might bear little resemblance to the mother tongue or even other isolated-group languages. This is a combination of speculation and logic, of course, but it seems reasonable, and I hope will contribute to the ongoing debate on this subject.

Borders are important in the development of different races and languages. They provide a means of separation and isolation, allowing differences in race and language to be developed and maintained. Traditionally, borders were more of a cultural and linguistic divide than a checkpoint as they are in most countries today. They are also used as defensive positions in case of attack from an outside enemy.[38]

Since Innocents would have no enemies, there would be no need to have defensive borders like we have. Instead, the Innocent's borders would be confined to geological formations, such as mountains, rivers, lakes, and oceans. Innocent's borders would not be something that is meant to keep people out but something to be overcome. Once overcome, the Innocent's world would become porous. Over time, this porousness would facilitate a joining and melding of cultures resulting in a dissolving of racial and linguistic differences. Eventually, the Innocents would become one race, one colour, and one language. The skin colour of the Innocents would probably be on the order of a medium tan. I wonder though, what would be their common language?

Having just explored the origins of race, skin colour, and language, it is hard to believe that people regard each other with trepidation simply because they look different or speak a different language. But then, that's our world.

POLITICS

Would there be politicians? Innocents would pride themselves on their political acumen. With their mutual respect for each other, they would have no trouble having a successful career as a politician. They would be of the highest integrity, with honesty their byword. To be recognized as a politician is to be admired.

Motivated by the precept of bringing no harm to another, governments around the world would create a congenial international climate, facilitating many worthwhile and beneficial agreements. These would make for a smoothly running world.

What forms of government would there be? Governments are necessary to serve and control the people.[39] But what kind of government? With the Innocents inherent respect for each other, their choice of government would likely be democratic.

Would they have multiple governments or just one world government? The tendency in our world is to form trading blocs in order to stay competitive. As these blocs become bigger, they begin to envelope continents. NAFTA and the European Union are examples.[40] With the concentration of wealth and power and the need for oversight and control, some form of government will need to exist in order to ensure that competition is fair. So, the trend in our world is probably towards a one-world government.

Since Innocents would probably have only one type of government, i.e. democratic, as well as their being of one race, one colour, one language, and borderless, their aim would naturally be a one-world government. From this perspective, the Innocent's world would lend itself more easily to a single government than in our world where we have many types of government, some corrupt, some not, but each claiming its part of the planet. How to get these governments to give up some of their power for the sake of international cooperation, is a challenge in our world.

Would there be Communism? Communism originated as a response to the massive channeling of wealth into the hands of a few. People lived in extreme poverty while the rich held parties.[41] Communism has always been an option for the poor and oppressed. In the Innocent's world there would be no unfair distribution of wealth and thus no desperately poor or oppressed since that would represent harm to another Innocent. Thus, there would be no need for communism.

Would Innocents engage in protests, sit-ins, strikes? Protests, sit-ins, and strikes are essentially unionesque actions to protest a perceived injustice. I would be surprised if a situation in the Innocent's world ever got to this stage. In keeping with their desire not to harm each other, which would include economic harm, Innocents would thoughtfully reach a compromise that is acceptable to all affected parties before that happened.

This thoughtful approach to potentially acrimonious situations suggests that Innocents place a greater emphasis on their logical ability rather than emotion in resolving disputes. Without the option of harming another to settle disagreements, as we tend to do, Innocents would be forced to develop their intellect in order to manage their world. This leads me to speculate on how the Innocent's brain and IQ might evolve over time. Would the cerebral cortex become more prominent, reflecting a higher IQ? Would the overall size of the brain increase and subsequently the skull that houses it?

There is research to show that overall brain size, particularly outer cortical thickness, positively relates to intelligence. Researchers used MRIs (Magnetic Resonance Imaging) to view those regions of the brain showing larger than normal volumes. They found that the outer cortex tended towards higher volumes in those with higher IQs.[42] Therefore, it seems probable that the Innocents would develop higher IQs, bigger brains, and thus larger heads, in response to their environment when considered over a geological timeframe.

FAMILY AND RELATIONSHIPS

Would Innocents know how to raise children properly? Would they, no matter how busy they were, always have time for their children? Would they never use the television, cellphone, or computer to act as babysitter to their children? Would they never abuse them?

Properly raised offspring are essential to the survival of a species. However, in our world of the Guilty, both parents need to work to make ends meet.[43] This leaves little time for their children. The traditional nuclear family is being destroyed by competitiveness and greed. It's not the children's fault, they're just innocent victims in a world of dwindling time and resources.

Lack of family cohesiveness is at the heart of many problems facing the world today. Single parenting is compounding the stresses a person normally faces in the workday world. These contribute to feelings of helplessness and frustration that are inevitably transmitted to our children. Crime, bullying, alcohol and drug addiction are frequently the offspring of distressed or absent families; and with more families breaking up as a result, many children feel lost and abandoned.[44]

Since God had originally created a bountiful world,[45] the Innocents would have abundant resources. Families could survive easily on just one salary and children would be taken care of with time to spare. Family structure would be more easily maintained with divorce less frequent. Exceedingly high intelligence, a commitment not to harm, and excellent negotiating skills should translate into the kind of caring sufficient to raise children successfully. Thus, Innocent children should grow up well-adjusted and able to create healthy families of their own. Growing up in the Innocent's world would be a rewarding and fulfilling experience.

Would women be willing to take a more assertive role in relationships with men, such as asking a man out on a date? Men come equipped with their own Achilles Heel, so to speak. It's their testicles. It's as if God decided that because He made males stronger than females, He ought to balance that out by making men particularly vulnerable to a well-placed kick. That is the situation in our world of the Guilty. In the Innocent's world, defending herself against a male aggressor would not be a concern since men, like women, do not wish to harm anyone. Innocent women would be free to openly appraise and consider their male prospects without fear.

Would Innocents lie to each other? They could tell white lies, lies that don't harm anyone, a dictum that rules the lives of Innocents. On the other hand, would Innocents always tell the truth? Again, because of their dictum not to harm another, they might choose not to be brutally honest for the sake of another's feelings. In all other situations an Innocent would invariably tell the truth.

Would there be bullies in an Innocent world? Schoolyard bullies often grow up into adult bullies that evolve different tactics to deal with their social problems.[46] Bullying is a wish to harm another and wouldn't be permitted in the world of the Innocent. Indeed, Innocents couldn't conceive of bullying one another.

Would Innocents have mistresses and misters? Mistresses and misters(?) indirectly hurt others, so they wouldn't be part of an Innocent's lifestyle. In fact, they wouldn't even know what the words mean. What are misters, anyway?

Would Innocents get angry at each other? Would they hate each other? Anger can be perceived as an assault and therefore destructive in its effect. It doesn't matter if the anger is only meant to show that you are upset, it is how it may be perceived by the individual receiving your anger. From that point of view, the anger is potentially detrimental, and since there is intention behind it, it must be considered evil. Hate is a more passive-aggressive form of anger, thus neither would exist in an Innocent's world.

Would they have divorce? Everyone makes mistakes, even Innocents. When it comes to love, we're all fallible. Yes, Innocents would have divorce, but only by mutual agreement. There would be no adultery, since that would harm another person. Child custody could be an issue, though.

ALCOHOL AND DRUGS

Alcohol and drugs have become a problem in our world of the Guilty. The global average consumption of pure alcohol (ethanol) is 6.4 litres per capita annually. Of the 194 WHO (World Health Organization) member countries, Belarus (formerly of the Soviet Union) ranks first at 17.5 litres per capita. In fact, based on regional averages, the heaviest drinkers in the world are almost exclusively from former member states of the USSR. Beyond the Soviet Union, UK ranks 25th at 11.6, Canada 40th at 10.2, while the U.S. stands at 48th at 9.2 litres per person, all well above the global average.[47]

As for illicit drugs, the worst country for opiate addiction is Afghanistan - the major supplier of opium from which heroin is derived - at 2.7% of the population. That's what can happen when you sample your own product. Its next door neighbour, Iran, is not far behind at 2.3%.[48] In the U.S., the rate is 3.8% for prescription drug abuse, particularly relating to opioid usage.[49] In Canada, our drug of choice is marijuana at 12.6% of the population.[50] Those are uncomfortable stats to deal with. It means that, on average, there is a reasonable chance the people you meet on any street are either overmedicated, drunk, stoned, or soon will be. Makes me wonder about our and our children's safety at the hands of these people.

Would Innocents drink alcohol? Alcohol is used as a drug and as such can be abused. Why would an Innocent need alcohol? One of the reasons people give for drinking alcohol is to make them feel more comfortable in social situations, to overcome feelings of apprehension and anxiety.[51] Would Innocents feel these emotions in social situations?

Imagine yourself an Innocent. You've just been invited to a party with people who are, for the most part, new to you. As an Innocent, how would you feel about that? Would you be apprehensive, even anxious? Apprehension and anxiety are fear-based emotions which are usually triggered in situations that are perceived as threatening to some degree. As an Innocent, you know you have nothing to fear from your fellow Innocents, and so, should not need alcohol.

Of course, there are situations where alcohol may be used to cope with the anxiety relating to stressful or frustrating events, such as a lost child, an accident, a failed promotion. So, alcohol might be consumed by Innocents, but only under certain circumstances.

Would there be Innocent alcoholics? Alcoholism has been described as a disease, a physical compulsion, or a mental obsession.[52] Whichever description fits, alcoholism is life-harming. It harms those that are addicted as well as those who love the addicted. It has the potential to harm any number of people, even innocent bystanders. If it only affected the addicted, it wouldn't be much of a problem. The alcoholic can drink him/herself to death for all anyone else may care. The problem is, we are not islands, we exist in a social network, which is especially true in Innocent society, so any self-destructive behaviour that an individual engages in, inevitably affects others. And since Innocents do not wish to harm each other, they would not drink to the point of alcoholism.

Regarding drugs, there are basically two types: medicinal and illicit. Most drugs start out being used as medicine.[53] It's only later when they are abused and a greater supply is needed than can be obtained from legitimate sources that they become illicit. Of course, there are illicit drugs that don't start out as medicine, the manufacture and distribution of which requires a more sophisticated network of supply.

Unfortunately, that is what happens in our world, the world of the Guilty. In the Innocent's world, with the physically rejuvenating power of the Tree of Life, medical drugs would be of very limited use. You will see in the next chapter what situations would require the use of medical drugs.

Would Innocents use illicit drugs? To use illicit drugs is to risk addiction. What is drug addiction? The National Institute of Drug Abuse defines drug addiction as a "chronic, relapsing brain disease that is characterized by compulsive drug seeking and use, despite harmful consequences. It is considered a brain disease because drugs change the brain; they change its structure and how it works. These brain changes can be long lasting and can lead to many harmful, often self-destructive, behaviors."[54]

Given the physically restorative power of the Tree of Life to return the brain to normal functioning, problems of drug addiction would not present themselves in the Innocent's world. Illicit drugs have the potential to cause harm to the user, thus there would no illicit drug suppliers, since that would contravene their dictum not to harm another. Therefore, Innocents would not be users of illicit drugs.

MEDICAL AND PHYSIOLOGY

In the Innocent's world would there be disease? Where does disease come from? Disease originates from one or both of two sources. One is external to the body and consists of an inappropriate reaction to something in the environment. The body is constantly exchanging matter with its environment, and if a particular piece of matter is something that the body can't accommodate or excrete, it manifests a diseased state. The other source of disease is internal to the body and constitutes a failure of the body mechanisms to operate properly, which may be genetic or age related.[55]

All disease in the Innocent's world, whether internal or external in origin, would be cured with the fruit of the Tree of Life. Thus, Innocents would be practically disease free.

Would Innocents have a healthy immune system? Since Innocents would be exposed to diseases, although ultimately cured by the Tree of Life, their immune systems should be robust to the point of being able to mount a quick defence against any recurring diseases. Thus, Innocents should not have to keep visiting the Tree of Life every time they get infected.

When God created humans and the universe, I'm sure He had it in mind that eventually His Innocents would venture out to the planets. Though the Innocents would be protected from diseases of their own planet, they may not be on other planets. I recall the movie *War of the Worlds* where the alien invaders were overcome by a tiny microbe. It always struck me as peculiar that these highly advanced invaders hadn't thought about that possibility beforehand. As interplanetary voyagers, Innocents would surely protect themselves from alien diseases before setting foot on a new planet. Even today's travellers vaccinate themselves when travelling to certain foreign countries.

It is possible that the Innocents could take a Tree of Life with them on their interplanetary journeys, but questions arise. One, would the Innocent's Tree of Life be effective against the diseases of an alien planet? The planet's diseases may be so different that the Tree of Life may not have the capability to cure the Innocent of an alien disease. Two, if the Innocents intended to colonize the planet, would the Tree of Life be able to grow in the planet's soil? Remember, the Tree of Life originates and flourishes in the Innocent's own planet's ecosystem, and may not do well in an alien environment.

Of course, these questions may be moot since God would still be available to help solve the problem. He could simply plant a new Tree of Life on the alien planet. Or, with their exceedingly high intelligence the Innocents could mutate their own Tree of Life through genetic engineering to accommodate the new environment. A third possibility is that the Tree of Life is ultimately adaptable and can live in any habitable environment and able to cure an Innocent of any disease the universe has to throw at them. That sounds like something God would make happen. In any case, Innocents should have no difficulty colonizing other planets.

Would there be Innocents who choose to stay young? As we, the Guilty, get older, we might reminisce about our younger days and how it was so much better than now. We may not remember that our youth was replete with misjudgement, risk, and naiveté. Our body's needs ruled our behaviour and, as a result, we sometimes got into trouble.

Innocents would have the option to remain at any age they choose by simply attending to the Tree of Life at the age they wish to stay. This is accomplished by first letting oneself grow to the age one wants by not eating the fruit of the Tree of Life. Then, when one has reached the desired age, begin attending the Tree of Life from that time forward. This means that the Tree of Life is not the fabled Fountain of Youth, but a Life Sustainer, maintaining the body, pain free, at the age one wants to be.

Would Innocents have perfect eyesight? There is no reason to think that younger Innocents would not have perfect eyesight, especially with periodic visits to the Tree of Life to correct any physical problems that may arise. However, eyesight tends to diminish as one gets older. If an Innocent chose to remain at an older age, then s/he could expect there to be some deterioration in their eyesight. Then again, there might not be any deterioration. With more frequent visits to the Tree of Life, eyesight may not be a problem for the elderly Innocents.

Would Innocents have good attention? What would that be like? With no guilt and virtually no pain to draw their attention inward, that suggests Innocents would have more attention available to focus outward. There is research to show that outward attention is negatively affected by pain.[56] Whether that pain is physical or emotional makes little difference. Indeed, emotional pain can be treated with the same medication, i.e. pain killers, that are used to treat physical pain.[57] Guilt can also have a detrimental effect on outward attention.[58] Therefore, given the guilt and pain we have to contend with, it seems likely that the Innocents would have higher outward attention capabilities than we do. Over geological time, how would this high attention translate physiologically?

Since there is no research on this topic that I can draw from, I am free to speculate as to any physical changes that might occur to the Innocent's body because of their heightened outward attention. Therefore, I will surmise that increased outward attention would generate increased visual data input via the eyes, thus demanding a need for greater optical capacity. This would probably mean larger eyes as well as greater brain processing capacity, resulting in a larger visual cortex.

There is an analogy that I would like to present in support of my speculation above. It is somewhat crude, but I think it will get the idea across. My analogy is the car engine. Normally, a small car has a small engine. However, if you put a big, powerful engine in this small car, you will overburden the drivetrain. In order to take full advantage of the power output of this big engine, you must upgrade your drivetrain - which includes the tires - to accommodate the greater stresses that will occur. The drivetrain has to be "beefed up", that is, it has to be constructed with stronger parts and materials, including larger tires. The impetus to this reconstruction of the drivetrain is the increased size of the engine.

Analogously, the impetus to the need for larger eyes and subsequently larger visual cortex is the greater outward attention that the Innocent would be capable of. Think of this greater attention as if it were a bigger and more powerful car engine. The Innocent's greater attention would create the need to "beef up" the downstream processing of visual data which would include the eyes and the visual cortex. The result is larger eyes and a thicker visual cortex.

Imagine having such great attention that you notice everything, even the individual grains of sand on the beach. Your panorama would be incredibly textured and detailed, colours brighter and more vibrant.

What kind of memory would Innocents have? There are many parts of the brain that are involved in memory production: the hippocampus, cerebellum, amygdala, thalamus, and the cerebral cortex, which includes the frontal, temporal, parietal, and occipital lobes.[59] Given that Innocents would have greater outward attention capabilities, and couple this with the need to "beef up" the downstream processing of the enormous amounts of data generated by this heightened attention - which must translate into highly detailed memories - these brain structures would be highly developed, resulting in increased size. In order to accommodate all this information, the Innocent's brain would have to expand, and subsequently the cranium that houses it.

Since this greater attention must include the five senses of sight, hearing, touch, smell, and taste, there are more opportunities to create memory triggers (reminders of a memory that are captured in a current event). With more memory triggers available there would exist more opportunities to recall a particular memory. Thus, Innocents should have a greater ability to recall memories.

Phenomenal multi-sense attention coupled with highly developed memory processing brain structures means Innocents should have excellent memories. Of course, Innocents can get distracted and some memory loss may result, but compared to our attention span, Innocents would be able to accommodate most distractions and still retain a good memory of an event.

In our world there are many documented causes for poor memory such as lack of sleep, underactive thyroid, alcohol, medication, stress, anxiety, and depression.[60] In the Innocent world, an underactive thyroid would be cured with the fruit of the Tree of Life. Also, alcohol would not be an issue in this world, as previously determined. You will see later in this chapter that medication would be a small part of any Innocent treatment program and as such should not be a cause for poor memory. Finally, it is hard to imagine Innocents having an issue with depression given their nature. The last three causes of poor memory: lack of sleep, stress, and anxiety are possible if, for example, an Innocent's child has gone missing or has had an accident. Thus Innocents would have few causes, if any, for poor memory.

Would Innocents have traumas to deal with? The word trauma is used to describe experiences or situations that are emotionally painful and distressing, and overwhelm a person's ability to cope, leaving them feeling powerless. Trauma is not an objective term; it is highly subjective. One person may have difficulty coming to terms with a traumatic event in their life, while another accepts it easily. It depends on their life experience and their thoughts about it as to how effectively they can deal with a traumatic event.[61]

Since there is no war, terrorism, murder, rape, or any of the other dastardly deeds we, the Guilty, tend to get up to, an Innocent would not have the occasion to be traumatized from those sources. However, an Innocent may have an accident severe enough that - although the physical injury would be repaired by use of the Tree of Life - s/he may become emotionally affected to such an extent they may feel traumatized. Therefore, though the sources of traumatization are greatly reduced, Innocents may still become traumatized.

Would Innocents have mental illness? What constitutes a mental illness, anyway? The New South Wales Law Foundation defines mental illness as "a condition characterized by the presence of symptoms such as delusions, hallucinations, a serious disorder of thought form, a severe disturbance of mood, sustained or repeated irrational behaviour which seriously impairs, either temporarily or permanently, the mental functioning of a person."[62] I don't mean to be overly technical here, but some people are apprehensive concerning the subject of mental illness, so I wanted to define it in as precise a manner as possible, to avoid any misunderstanding.

Mental illness is caused by a combination of biological, psychological, and environmental factors:[63]

Biological factors include a brain defect or injury, genetics, infections, exposure to toxins, poor nutrition, and long term drug abuse. Except for long term drug abuse, all biological factors would be remedied with a visit to the Tree of Life. As previously determined, Innocents would not be addicted to drugs, so long term drug abuse would not be a cause of mental illness.

Psychological factors are listed as emotional, physical, or sexual abuse, neglect, and an important early loss. In Innocent society there would be no such thing as emotional, physical, or sexual abuse, or even neglect, since those would constitute harm to another. Regarding an important early loss, such as losing a parent, that is possible since there would still be accidents and natural disasters. However, given the caring nature of the Innocents, the emotional loss would be relieved, more so than in our world. The proverb "It takes a village to raise a child" is never truer than in the Innocent's world.

Environmental factors that contribute to mental illness in our world are dysfunctional family life, parental drug abuse, unrealistic social or cultural expectations, death, divorce, and changing jobs or schools.

Dysfunctional family life would not exist in the Innocent's world as pointed out in the previous chapter "Family and Relationships". Parental drug abuse would also not exist for reasons already outlined. Unrealistic social and cultural expectations, for example, our equivalence of thinness to beauty that has led to cases of anorexia in our world; I don't see Innocents adopting unrealistic expectations of their members, certainly not to the point of developing a mental illness. The very idea of expecting an Innocent to act in a manner that is contrary their own sense of mental and physical wellbeing represents an indirect form of harm and would not be permitted in Innocent society.

Death would be such a rare occurrence in the Innocent's world that it probably would come as more of shock to the inhabitants than in our world. As such, Innocents might find it more difficult to accept someone's death, particularly if that someone is a loved one. In our world, death is so common that we have ritualized it with funerals and memorials, to the point that, perhaps, our expressions of sympathy have also become ritualized to some degree.

Not so in the Innocent's world. The Innocents outpouring of sympathy would be genuine and heartfelt. The Innocent griever would feel that love and be uplifted by it. Death would bring a coming together of the community with such a focus of sympathy and compassion that the sufferer could not help but be soothed and comforted. As a result, the griever should not suffer any mental illness due to their loss.

With the Innocent's inherent caring nature, divorce would be infrequent. Divorce that does occur would be reached amicably since the partners do not wish to harm each other. Thus, there would be no mental health issues at the spousal level. For the children of divorce, once again I refer to the above proverb.

Just as the effects of a trauma depend on the person experiencing it, any mental health issues arising from changing jobs or schools must also depend on the individual. That being said, given the caring attitude of Innocents towards themselves and others, and in particular their healthy family upbringing, it is hard to believe an Innocent would be negatively affected to the point of suffering from a mental illness simply from changing a job or school.

Except for the physical sources, and those are cured with the Tree of Life, all of the above causes for mental illness are the result of stress or shock to the psyche. As noted throughout my argument, it is the caring nature and upbringing of the Innocents that enables an Innocent to recover from that stress or shock, so that no mental illness should occur. Therefore, given all of the above, I conclude that Innocents should have no mental health issues.

Would Innocents have worries, anxieties, and frustrations? Though Innocent parents wouldn't have to worry about their children being abducted by a sexual predator, they would probably worry about their children getting lost, or having accidents, or not doing well in school. So, Innocents would worry.

What about anxieties? Fear of flying might be one of them. It takes a tremendous amount of trust to hand your life over to a complete stranger who is supposedly competent to fly a plane that is composed of about a million parts, any one of which could fail and possibly send the plane plummeting to earth. Yes, I would say that any right thinking Innocent would be at least wary of flying in a plane.

Would Innocents get frustrated? The problems that might frustrate an Innocent would be greater than our own. Problems like inventing a stellar propulsion drive, or getting all countries of the world to agree on a proposal and not just the G20 or, everyone's favourite, dealing with a teenager. Yes, I would say that even Innocents could get frustrated.

Would Innocents experience moments of insanity? This is good question. Would not a parent who has lost a child to some horrific accident go, momentarily at least, insane with grief? I think even for an Innocent that would be entirely possible.

Would an Innocent know fear? Would Innocents be afraid of each other? Of course not. They all care about each other. However, the kind of fear that comes from realizing your child is missing is something Innocents would have to contend with, just as we do.

Would there exist Innocents with disabilities? No, absolutely not. Not with the Tree of Life available to all.

Would there be dentists or optometrists? With the Tree of Life to provide perfect teeth and eyesight, Innocents wouldn't need these services.

Would there be doctors? There would be doctors of general medicine, someone to take care of the Innocent's aches and pains, at least until their next visit to the Tree of Life. Doctors in the Innocent's world would not have training beyond that needed to treat ailments resulting from accidents such as lacerations and broken bones. No doctors would exist for the treatment of non-accident related disorders such as ulcers, cancers, tumours, and the like, since there wouldn't be any with the Tree of Life available to cure the patient of these medical maladies. The training period for doctors would be correspondingly less, probably something like six months to a year. Doctors would not be the demigods that they are here in the world of the Guilty.

Would there be Big Pharma? With doctors treating only accident related injuries, there is probably not much need for medication beyond pain killers, muscle relaxants, anesthetics, and antiseptics. Morphine might be used in the more serious cases. With the Tree of Life available in practically every neighbourhood, the Innocent's "Emergency" might be the Tree of Life or the nearest doctor's office, whichever is closer.

Would there be fat Innocents? I don't have a problem with a person being fat and doubt that Innocents would either. In fact, in the past, being fat was considered an indicator of how well a tribe was surviving. If they were wealthy enough to be able to waste their resources in gluttonous behaviour, then it showed that theirs was a tribe worth being associated with. If an Innocent is happy with their weight, I don't see that visits to the Tree of Life would automatically change that condition. Being the image of God does not necessarily mean that you will have a perfect body. It has more of a spiritual connection than that.

Would there be old Innocents? As a 77-year old, I can relate to this question, and possibly answer it. Old age has been greatly denigrated on this planet of the Guilty. Nobody here wants to get old, even though there are benefits to being over the hill. You are calmer, things don't bother you as much. You don't get interrupted by thinking about sex and its various entanglements. Your mind is more peaceful, leaving way to pause and reflect. For the peace of mind, the Innocents might choose to be older. Besides, the Tree of Life will take care of all their physical complaints.

What would their medical systems be like? With the Tree of Life readily available, any medical system that the Innocents might have would be rudimentary at best.

This is unlike in our world where we have some medical systems that, ironically, cause people to be sicker than they otherwise would be. Here in Canada, for example, we have so-called free universal-access medical, called Medicare.

It is anything but free; it is paid for through our taxes and monthly premiums. Even the medicine isn't free. Moreover, with its seemingly interminable wait lists, accessibility becomes a relative question.

Canada is notorious for its long wait times for medical treatment. Our constant struggle to get timely health care in a medical system that utilizes a triage approach in deciding who gets treated first, coupled with the long wait times, results in patients, on average, becoming sicker longer.[64][65] A medical system like this makes a mockery of the term "healthcare". Unfortunately, this is a type of medical system we have to deal with here in the world of the Guilty.

SPORTS AND RECREATION

What kind of sports would Innocents enjoy? Certainly not boxing with its brutality, and probably not football or hockey with all that padding to hopefully keep one safe from harm. No, none of the physically punishing sports, but non-contact sports like tennis, basketball, or golf. Baseball might be good although probably too boring for the Innocent's taste. There are many sporting activities that Innocents would enjoy that don't require regular visits to the hospital.

Would Innocents engage in risky behaviour, like car racing or parachute jumping? Since the cost (loss of immortal life) far outweighs the benefit (thrill of overcoming one's fear), I don't see Innocents engaging in any unnecessarily risky behaviour. This begs the question: Why do we, the Guilty, engage in unnecessarily risky behaviour?

What about gambling? Gambling as a form of recreation wouldn't be a problem in the Innocent's world. However, gambling in order to make up for past losses could be an issue. Gambling is a thrill-seeking activity, an effort to get high, in a manner of speaking. Gambling is not logical, for the House has the advantage. So why do it? Lives have been ruined because of gambling. Gambling has the potential to cause harm to the participant, including those who depend on the gambler. If a person's gambling got to a point where livelihoods were negatively affected, then it falls into the category of compulsive gambling, which is thought to be either a mental illness or an addiction. The Mayo Clinic defines compulsive gambling as "the uncontrollable urge to keep gambling despite the toll it takes on your life."[66] Compulsive gambling is a self-destructive activity.

Whether considering compulsive gambling from a mental health standpoint or simply as an addiction, no gambling services would exist to support their habit since that would constitute harm to another Innocent. And since gambling services would have to exist for the recreational gamblers, there can be no compulsive gamblers. Therefore, recreational gambling might be engaged in but not to the point of compulsivity.

Would they have martial arts? Many martial arts today are sporting activities that are combative in nature, thus would not be tolerated in the world of the Innocents. However, there are martial arts that are strictly meditative or have a meditative component, for example, Aikido or Tai Chi. Those forms of martial arts would be seen by Innocents as beneficial.

POVERTY

Would Innocents have the poor, the homeless? Being poor could be a choice that some Innocents might make. They may choose a lifestyle that requires fewer material possessions and thus less expense. They may want to be free from excess responsibilities and obligations. They may not want to work so that they can pursue occupations that are not necessarily income generating. They may want to pursue art for art's sake, for example, and not as a means of support. There are different reasons for choosing to be poor.

Would there be involuntary poverty? As pointed out in the previous chapter on agriculture, there would probably exist impoverished regions on the Innocent's planet due to economic underdevelopment. However, Innocents being who they are, a joint effort would be made to develop these regions as quickly as possible in order to reduce the negative economic impact on its citizenry.

What if an Innocent had an accident that left him/her permanently disabled? With access to the physically regenerative power of the Tree to Life, an Innocent would be cured of the disability. Being disabled for an eternity would be cruel and God wouldn't allow that. Therefore, voluntary poverty might exist but not otherwise.

Homelessness is an extreme form of poverty and given the generosity of the Innocent's welfare system many of the causes for homelessness would be avoided. One of the reasons for this generous welfare is the availability of funds recouped from no military spending, since there would be no war. As an example, for the United States alone, converting all military spending into welfare spending could virtually double what the average welfare recipient would receive.[67]

In our world there are certain contributing factors that can lead to homelessness:[68]

- Lack of affordable housing: House prices, like all things economic, are subject to the rules of supply and demand. Looking at the supply side, it is reasonable to expect that with an ample supply of source materials, which God has ensured would be abundant, coupled with a readily available labour force, new housing in the Innocent's world would not be in short supply, thereby keeping prices reasonable.

What about existing housing? Would Innocents allow house resale prices to climb so high as to leave most Innocents unable to afford them? No, of course not. Innocents would not let greed motivate them to seek the highest price possible for a house if they see that it would indirectly result in Innocents becoming homeless. High house prices tend to translate into high rental rates, which is something that would affect the homeless. Therefore, there would be no lack of affordable housing, and thus not a contributor to homelessness in the Innocent's world.

- Poor physical or mental health: Generally, poor physical health has different causes than poor mental health, so they will be dealt with separately here.

  Poor physical health would not persist with the Tree of Life available to rejuvenate the sufferer. As determined earlier, poor mental health would not be found in the Innocent's world and, therefore, would not be a contributing factor to homelessness.

- Gambling addiction, as well as drug and alcohol problems, would not be found among the Innocents, so those would not contribute to homelessness either.

- Family and relationship breakdown: Not all love relationships are made in heaven and even the

Innocents might have problems in this area. However, given the caring attitude that Innocents would have for each other, no one would find themselves homeless as a result of a broken relationship.

- Domestic Violence: No such thing in the Innocent's world and therefore not a cause of homelessness.

- Physical and Sexual Abuse: These are intentional abuses that would not exist in the Innocent's society.

Homelessness would not be an issue in the Innocent's world since there would be nothing to fear about bringing a homeless person into one's home. With no crime, no drug addiction, and no mental health issues, a homeless person living with an Innocent should not present a problem. And their stay would not be prolonged since it would just be a matter of finding appropriate housing for the individual. With the Innocent's generous welfare program, which would include housing, the homeless person would not be homeless for long.

Therefore, given the above, there is no reason for any Innocent to find him/herself homeless. It is unfortunate that is not the case in our world.

MEDIA

News reporting in our world has become big business. In a very real sense, the Fourth Estate has lost its direction as well as its directive: to report the news honestly and without bias. News organizations operate as businesses and as such seem to place their bottom line at a higher level of priority than honest journalism.[69]

Beautiful, sexy anchorwomen host the nightly newscasts. Appearing intelligent and knowledgeable, it's an open question as to whether they are newswomen or actresses. And even if they aren't actresses, there are probably more capable but possibly less attractive newswomen that could host the broadcast. They would undoubtedly come across as more intelligent and knowledgeable than their beautiful counterparts.

In the Innocent's world, news would be reported factually and without bias, and without sex appeal. Would the news be boring, though? Depends on who's seeing it. If it's the bloodthirsty Guilty, then the Innocent's news reports would probably bore us to tears. However, you have to remember who would be viewing these news reports: Innocents. Think of the most boring parts of the Guilty's news and that is probably what interests the Innocent. "One man's trash is another man's art" probably expresses the basic difference between the two styles of journalism.

I've picked up a newspaper and I'm scrolling through it to see what might interest an Innocent. Of course, there might be articles not in our newspaper that Innocents may enjoy, but I have to start somewhere.

In our local rag, *The Vancouver Sun*, one headline reads "91% of seniors' facilities below staffing guideline, report says." Now this is something an Innocent might be interested in. It has human interest, management, and money issues to consider. The front page of this particular date doesn't carry some of the more violent fare that is usually expected. Must be a slow news day.

The Business section is mind-numbingly boring to me, but to the Innocents, probably captivating. Then there's the Sports section. This might be interesting to some of the less cerebral of the Innocents, those who like a little conflict in their read. Sorry, no hockey or football, fans, too violent for the Innocent's palate.

Usually I would find the Entertainment section next but not this time. Again, probably a slow news day. Last up in this paper is a combination section of Real Estate and Travel. I can see Innocents enjoying these, as we do, particularly if they are planning to buy or sell property or if travel plans are in the offing.

So, that's what might interest the Innocent if they were to pick up our newspaper off the newsstand. There may be more sections in their own newspaper that are popular with their readers, but I won't speculate on what those topics might be. That is specific to the taste and intelligence of the Innocent reader.

Would Innocents have tabloids? Of course they would. What person, Guilty or Innocent, doesn't enjoy a bit of gossip? Sometimes you can't get more accurate information on who's doing what to whom than in the tabloids.

RELIGION

Would the Innocent's world have disparate religious faiths worshipping the same god? Since Innocents would certainly have the power of choice, it is conceivable that different religious faiths might emerge. It is difficult to be decisive on this point because it is not obvious to me how various faiths that worship the same god can have such different approaches to their worship of Him. Indeed, in our world of the Guilty, we've even had religious conflicts - that are sometimes violent - arise between faiths that worship the same god; Muslims and Christians, for example.[70]

Would they have religious zealots? To be classified as a zealot one needs to be passionately devoted to a cause. In our world, the word "zealot" connotes something fanatical, even violent. However, in the Innocent's world, zealotry would not involve fanatical or violent behaviour but probably something approaching the prophetic. It is easy to envision some Innocents becoming so consumed in their love and worship of God, that they might be viewed as zealots.

Would there be Innocent atheists? I've shown that the Innocents wouldn't need the Ten Commandments to govern their lives. The first commandment says "Do not worship any other gods but Me." But it doesn't say you have to worship God. So, Innocents would be free not to worship God, if they chose. Indeed, they wouldn't have to believe in a god, any god. They have that freedom of choice. Thus, Innocents can choose to be atheists if they wish.

Would there be Innocent Buddhists? Buddha was an individual who lived about 2,500 years ago and taught what he called "a middle way" between sensual indulgence and severe asceticism. He did not believe in singular or multiple gods in the sense of someone to pray to. His focus was overcoming the urges of the body, with the goal of attaining spiritual enlightenment.[71] Since Buddhism doesn't require that you worship a god, then the first commandment is not broken. Thus, Buddhism may be a quasi-religious movement among the Innocents.

BUSINESS AND COMMERCE

Business has been around as long as man has needed to trade goods so to acquire those things another has in order to round out their lives. Commerce is the large scale evidence of business activity.

In our world, although business is generally beneficial, it can be cutthroat, potentially leaving businesses and lives in ruins. We can be so unfeeling when it comes to a competitor's interests. Putting a competitor out of business through one's own efforts is nothing to be proud of. Instead, such business owners should be ashamed.

Would there be business mergers? One of the reasons businesses merge is to drive out competition to secure a market. This means, however, that smaller competitors could be forced to lay off their employees. Newly merged businesses do not hire employees as a general rule, they usually divest of employees in an effort to streamline their operations. Thus, the net effect of a merger is a decrease in employee presence.[72] This decrease could have a detrimental effect on an Innocent's wellbeing, a subtle form of harm. For this reason, business mergers in order to increase market share would not be allowed in the world of the Innocents.

Would they have unions? In our world of the Guilty, trade unions were formed in the 19th century with a mandate to address wage and safety concerns.[73] Wages aside, imagine a world where your safety is not a concern to your employer. You have to threaten them with massive work stoppages before they will listen to you. Unfortunately, that is the world we live in.

In the world of the Innocents there would be no need for unions. Employers would put safety first for their employees. Minimizing wages is an attempt to maximize profit on the backs of the employees, something the Innocent employers would be averse to do, since it would represent an oblique form of harm to another Innocent.

Would Innocents have inflation or recession? There are two types of inflation: Demand-pull and Cost-push. Demand-pull inflation is where demand exceeds supply, where supply is in the form of products and services. As an example, if the Central Bank suddenly eases the money supply within the banking system, people will have more money available to spend, thus driving up demand. If businesses don't hire more employees or increase production to meet this demand, prices go up.

The other driver of inflation is called Cost-push. This is where the cost of supplying goods and services rises rapidly. This can be through increases in wages or the cost of input materials in the production process. Facing higher costs, businesses may lay off employees or slow production. With this type of inflation, supply is reduced relative to demand, again causing prices to rise. With both demand-pull and cost-push inflation, the economy is experiencing shocks that upset the balance of supply and demand.[74]

The major cause of a recession is high and persistent inflation in one or more products or services, particularly if those products or services are significant to the overall economy, such as energy or housing. As prices rise, individuals and businesses are able to purchase a smaller percentage of these products and services. As prices continue to rise, individuals and businesses may redirect any discretionary funds they possess towards saving rather than spending. Businesses may do this by laying off employees, lowering wages, or cutting production. Individuals may do this by putting their money into bank savings instruments or government bonds, looking for a return that is stable and guaranteed. These cost-cutting and saving efforts, if strong enough, could result in a recession where wages and prices fall in an economy of lower production and demand.

Employees lose their jobs, companies go bankrupt, and government support payments increase.[75]

Could these two economic conditions, inflation and recession, occur in the Innocent's economy? Given the detrimental effect inflation and recession can have on their lives, Innocents would make it a priority to ensure that these situations are mitigated so no drastic economic fluctuations occur. To completely eliminate inflation or recession is impossible; only good oversight and control can lessen the problems that ensue from these two forces.

Would Innocents have financial crises? Why do we have financial crises? There are many factors that can lead to a financial crisis, not the least of which are greed and miscalculation.[76] The 2008 Global Financial Crisis that brought the financial systems of our world to their knees was avoidable. There were warnings of an impending crisis but none were heeded.[77] Given the high intelligence and logical ability the Innocents possess, they would avoid the financial crises we seem unable to.

What about the stock market, bonds, futures? Investing is one thing, gambling another. Investing in the stock market is an investment in people, the people with the ideas and the commitment to make a successful business. Investing in bonds is similar in that you are giving money to someone, but what they do with it is their business. As a bondholder, the only rights you have is the expectation that at some future date you will get your money back, plus interest. Putting money into futures is neither of those things. It is similar to gambling.[78] Not much different than if you were betting the horses. And this is where it can get tricky, and addictive. No, I don't see futures purchases as an activity that Innocents would engage in. It is fraught with risk and possible addiction that might prove detrimental to the Innocent's wellbeing.

Would there be Innocent workaholics? Why are there workaholics anyway? Why does a person choose to spend time at work when s/he could be spending that time with family or engaging in recreational activities? Whatever the reason, workaholism is an obsessive type of behaviour, which is viewed as having either a mental health or an addictive cause. Workaholism is a destructive activity that jeopardizes relationships and even the workaholic's health.[79]

My argument against alcoholism among Innocents was a social one; that we exist as part of a social network and any self-destructive behaviour we engage in inevitably affects others. For that reason there would be no alcoholic Innocents. The same argument applies to workaholics. If there are any individuals who would have a close social network, it would be the Innocents; their caring nature for each other would demand it. Thus, any of their members that engage in self-destructive behaviour would be felt throughout the network. Like a spider's web, any disturbance in the peace of the social web is immediately transmitted to the occupants. Their response would be so quick and caring that alcoholism and workaholism would not have a chance to take hold.

POPULATION

Since the Innocents would be immortal, how would they control the size of the population? Population becomes an issue when there is not enough food.[80] Our world has only 10% arable land, and with our population continuing to grow, eventually population pressure will become a critical issue. As previously surmised, virtually all of the Innocent's world would be arable, thus making population control not a great concern, at least for a while. Besides, with the Innocent's phenomenal intelligence and plenty of money recouped from no military spending, they would have used population pressure as the impetus to finding a way off the planet for colonization purposes. Super high IQ and lots of money: the ideal combination for solving many problems.

Excluding Antarctica, we have 143 million square kilometres (35.336 billion acres) of land on Earth.[81] In order to survive, a person needs a minimum of 0.07 hectares (0.173 acres) of land.[82] If we assume that all the land is arable, including mountains and deserts, then the maximum population that can be supported works out to about 205 billion people. Note, this figure does not include food harvested from our oceans. However, from the point of view of this discussion's conclusions, the amount (17%) does not prove significant.[83]

Now, let's imagine the following scenario: under God's command to "fill the earth", Adam and Eve would have begun procreating children starting at puberty, around 16 years of age. With the Tree of Life readily available, Adam and Eve and their descendants would be immortal, so there is virtually no death rate to consider. I ran a calculation showing the size of the population based on the number of child-bearing couples, assuming a 50-50 gender split of offspring that grow up to child-bearing age, who then begin producing children of their own.

At 16 years of age, Adam and Eve begin producing say, one child every two years until menopause, about 32 years later, assuming Innocents have menopause when we do. With the Tree of Life available, they may not have menopause, but I have to limit their child production to a reasonable timeframe or the question of how many children a couple can realistically parent begins to superimpose itself on the calculation. Even 16 children seems too many, especially from the woman's perspective. However, this is just an exercise in order to give us a theoretical maximum. Whether or not it can actually be done is another question entirely.

First, let's look at the calculation for population size:

The 0th generation produces the 1st generation: Adam and Eve (the 0th generation) begin producing children (the 1st generation), one every two years, at age 16. By the time menopause is reached, they will have produced 16 children. Assuming a 50-50 gender split, that's 8 males and 8 females. Ignoring the moral issue, these offspring pair up, male and female, comprising 8 couples. First generation: 8 couples.

The 1st generation produces the 2nd generation: Each of the 8 couples of the 1st generation ultimately produce - at one child every two years and a 50-50 gender split - 8 more couples. Second generation: 8 x 8 couples = 8^2 couples.

The 2nd generation produces the 3rd generation: Continuing the above logic with the third generation we then have an outcome of 8^3 couples. And so on through to the 12th generation producing the 13th generation of 8^{13} couples. This is a power-sum series with 8 as the base:

$$1 + 8 + 8^2 + 8^3 + \dots + 8^{10} + 8^{11} + 8^{12}$$

$$+ 8^{13} = 6.282 \text{ x } 10^{11} \text{ couples.}$$

I've stopped at 8 to the power of 13 because the population of couples becomes enormous - over 628 billion couples, which translates into over 1.25 trillion people on Earth. That is well over the 205 billion people it is hypothesized that Earth is capable of supporting.

Now, let's calculate the time it takes to produce these 1.25 trillion people:

The central issue here is the time it takes to fully produce a particular generation. That time is how long it takes to produce the last child of that generation.

Adam and Eve start producing children at age 16 and continue until they are 48 years old. It has taken them 48 years to produce their last child. This is the 1st generation. Now, the time it takes for this 1st generation to produce its last child of the 2nd generation, i.e. to fully produce the 2nd generation, is the time it takes for the youngest couple (the last born) of the 1st generation to produce its last child, which is again 48 years. This process continues for each subsequent generation until the 13th generation is fully produced. This is a straight sum series with 48 as the base:

$$48 + 48 + 48 + 48 + 48 + 48 + 48 + 48 + 48 +$$
$$48 + 48 + 48 + 48 = 13 \times 48 = 624 \text{ years.}$$

So, if Innocent couples each religiously produce children at a rate of one child every two years, assuming a 50-50 gender split of offspring who then mate to produce more children, they would have produced over 1.25 trillion people in less than 625 years. Of course, these calculations are based on some morally dubious sibling relationships, but they can represent a theoretical maximum.

ART, MUSIC, WRITING, AND THEATRE

What would their art, music, books, and movies be like? The Innocent's art and entertainment would be beautiful, wondrous, and memorable. However, there would be no art or entertainment that is violent and very little born out of the suffering of the artist. In particular, books and movies would not have murder, war, rape, horror, gun fights, evil spirits, and so forth. Generally none of the dark, noir genre. Drama and romance might be popular with the Innocents. However, since Innocents would be great thinkers, movies of a more intellectual nature - documentaries and mysteries, are examples - would probably be the main source of video entertainment. Stand-up comedy and sitcoms would also be popular with the Innocents, although we Guilty might not get the jokes. The art and entertainment industry would be alive with fulfilling and emotionally satisfying experiences, more so than in our world.

Would Innocents have movie stars? No Claude Van Dam, Arnold Schwarzenegger, Steven Seagal, Sylvester Stallone, or Chuck Norris however, since they are associated with violence on the screen. Stars like Hugh Grant, Meryl Streep, Richard Gere, Tom Hanks, and Julia Roberts from genres such as romance, comedy, sci-fi, westerns, adventure, dramas, historical, and musicals, would be popular with the Innocents.

Would they have death metal rock? Heavy metal, sure, why not? Death metal with its connotation of death and destruction, would not be something the younger, teenage Innocents would enjoy.

Would there be graffiti? Some graffiti can be artful and would be tolerated and possibly even encouraged in Innocent society.

Would they have Blues music? It is with a certain sadness - no pun intended - that we must accept that Blues music, with its emphasis on the melancholy, would not be a part of the Innocent music scene. This brings to mind a philosophical point that Blues is meant to assuage the sad feelings of the listener by expressing the melancholy in such a beautiful way. It is sad - here I go again - that Innocents won't get to enjoy it.

SCIENCE AND TECHNOLOGY

What about science and technology? Would the Innocents create the atomic bomb? The atom bomb was developed to be the ultimate weapon. Then came the hydrogen bomb, which was even more powerful. We know that the nuclear bomb was not developed to satisfy our energy needs so much as to satisfy a lust for another kind of power. The bombings of Hiroshima and Nagasaki demonstrate that it didn't matter how many died who got in the way of that.[84]

However, developing nuclear power as a potential energy source might be something the Innocents would pursue but only if they could guarantee its safety. I can't imagine how they would guarantee the safety of their nuclear plants. But then, I'm not an Innocent.

The role of science is to investigate the natural world.[85] The aim of technology is to make living easier for people.[86]

Innocents would be interested in science and technology, as long as it benefits humanity.

With the Innocents incredibly high IQ, not to mention their not needing to spend money on the military, they would undoubtedly be well in advance of us in science and technology. They may have even reached the point in their scientific and technological development to be able to use the sun for all their energy needs. Utilizing the electromagnetic nature of sunlight, the Innocents would probably have found a way to directly power their cars, boats, planes, homes, businesses, everything. Indeed, solar energy is the most natural, the cleanest, and virtually inexhaustible form of energy that can be used.

The Unified Field Theory describes uniting the four basic forces of the universe: gravitation, electromagnetism, the strong and weak nuclear forces into different manifestations of one all-encompassing force. The strong nuclear force is responsible for the binding of protons and neutrons in the nucleus of an atom. The weak nuclear force is involved in radioactive decay.[87] The UF Theory would probably be fully developed and who knows what benefits could be derived from that, possibly a stellar propulsion drive.

On the subject of space exploration, with more money and resources available, coupled with population pressure concerns, the Innocents would be directed to space exploration earlier in their history than ours. I have calculated previously that the population of the Earth would reach unsustainable levels in a relatively short time given optimal production of offspring at a maximized rate. Of course, Innocents would take measures to address their population expansion, taking the necessary steps to relieve the pressure such as discovering new and more efficient methods of food production. They may have even perfected soilless plant growing, thus eliminating the need for arable land space.

Quantum mechanics, also known as quantum physics, concerns itself with the world of the very small, on the order of atoms and subatomic particles. In this quantum world, the existence of a particle is not a certainty. Indeed, a particle in this world can sometimes be a wave, and vice versa. Actually, not much is certain in the quantum universe. For example, of the location and speed of a particle/wave, only one can be known for sure, while the other is just a probability.[88]

However, the search for answers in the quantum universe has led to the discovery of quantum entanglement, where two entangled particles, though separated by a considerable distance, show simultaneous reactions when one or the other is acted upon.[89] This shows possibilities with teleportation: instantaneous transfer of objects from one location to another. If this outcome is possible then Innocents probably would have discovered it.

Digital computing, which requires that a computer bit be either '1' or '0', would have long since given way to quantum computing where a bit, called a qubit, can be either '1', '0', or both.[90] The quantum computer, utilizing the principles of quantum mechanics, would have the capability to be in multiple states, enabling it to perform tasks using all possible permutations simultaneously.[91] This greater computing power could lead to the solution of a great many scientific problems such as optimization, machine learning, or statistical sampling; basically any problem that is either too large or complex for regular digital computers.[92]

Nanotechnology is the science of manipulating atoms and molecules individually to construct useful products such as lightweight but strong materials, targeted chemotherapy that won't damage healthy cells, and more nutritious foods. A nanometer is one billionth of a meter with nanotechnology typically operating in the range of 1 to 100 nanometers. This makes for extremely minute manipulations. Atoms and molecules stick together because they have complementary shapes that lock or charges that attract. Imagine not having to rely on chemical or thermal processes to create something; you could use nanotechnology to create practically anything you want.[93][94]

Safe energy, interstellar travel, quantum mechanics, quantum computing, and nanotechnology are pursuits that Innocents would undoubtedly have long since mastered due to their larger brains and greater reasoning powers. Indeed, there are probably scientific and technological frontiers that we haven't even considered yet that Innocents would be well into solving.

LEGAL

Would there be laws? Laws of a society are categorized as either criminal or civil. The Innocents would have no criminal laws, since there would be no crime. What about civil laws? Civil laws exist primarily to resolve disputes between individuals.[95] As far as that goes, disputes between Innocents would not result in harm, so civil laws would be fairly benign.

Would they need rules of behaviour? Innocents would have such a high regard for each other that any activities that might harm another wouldn't even be considered. Activities that are risky to oneself like bungee jumping or parasailing, for example, may be undertaken, if just for the thrill of conquering one's fears. But then, engaging in risky behaviour for the sake of experiencing a thrill may not sit too well with the participant since s/he is risking their immortal life. That is a high price to pay. However, accidents do happen, so some rules of behaviour would probably exist in Innocent society to prevent that.

Would Innocents cheat on their taxes, defraud insurance companies, so-called victimless crimes? We in the world of the Guilty seem to have a threshold below which we view our crimes as victimless. We refuse to see the damage we cause because it seems so small as to be inconsequential. Tax evasion and insurance fraud are not victimless crimes. People are still negatively affected through higher taxes and higher insurance rates. Incidentally, also affected are those who commit these crimes. Innocents subscribe to a higher ethical standard that most of us can only dream of. So, no, Innocents would not engage in tax cheating or insurance fraud, indeed any activity that has the remotest chance of harming another, however minor.

Would they have courts to settle disputes? Criminal courts, no. Civil courts could be a forum for logical reasoning and discussion in order to reach agreement between opposing parties. This is the kind of forum that Innocents would excel at. A civil court process would be ideal for Innocents to come together with the objective of finding common ground.[96]

Would they have police since there is no crime? There are other functions that the police perform besides criminal law enforcement: social services, traffic and crowd control, protecting people from harm, are just a few.[97] There will always be a need for people who are there to help, direct, and protect those who need it. Police are the logical choice for that kind of function. There would be no firearms since the police wouldn't need them in the Innocent world.

Would they have lawyers? Our legal system has become so large and complex that is it sometimes difficult to avoid breaking some obscure law that is still on the books. It is ironic that we need lawyers to protect us from a system that is meant to protect us. We, the Guilty, have both criminal lawyers and civil lawyers. Innocents would not need criminal lawyers since there is no criminal law. However, they would still need civil lawyers to settle disputes. Attorneys dealing with civil law assist clients with litigation, trusts, contracts, mortgages, titles, leases, etc.[98] These are issues that would exist in the Innocent's world and thus lawyers would be needed to help their clients navigate the legal system.

THE RICH AND POWERFUL

In our world of the Guilty, it seems that we've always had the rich. They sit in their fancy palaces surveying their surroundings, perhaps imagining that they are actually in charge of all they see. Of course, it's pure fantasy on their part.

They scrabble and claw their way up, leaving anger and hate in their wake, driven by their need to be at the top of the heap. They don't care; money and power is all they want. Here is an interesting statistic: over 20%, that's one in five CEOs, are classified as psychopaths.[99] So, there is a reasonable chance your boss is someone pretending to be human.

We would be living in a very dangerous world if our leaders, those in power over us, were psychopaths. And how do we know that is not currently the case? We don't. Psychopaths are known for their charm and persuasiveness, so it's entirely possible that up to one in five politicians are psychopaths, as well.[100] Perhaps the only reason we haven't already gone up in nuclear smoke is the psychopath's own sense of survival.

Would there be rich Innocents? God wants His children to prosper, and as long as no one suffers as a result of that prosperity, there is no reason rich Innocents wouldn't exist.

Would there be an elitist element among the Innocents? Elitists are individuals who feel best equipped to run things, things like business, government, academia. These are people with a narcissistic view of themselves and their abilities. Since there is no intent to harm anyone - they just want to take over - there is no reason to think they have evil in them. Therefore, it is possible for elitist groups to form amongst the Innocents.

APPEARANCE AND PERSONALITY

What would Innocents look like? What would their personalities be like? I have discussed two physical characteristics elsewhere in this book. Innocents would have unfettered outward attention that is not drawn inward onto the guilt and pain that exists in our minds. Couple this increased attention with a necessary optical capacity to handle the visual data and we get large eyes and a thick visual cortex.

The other physical quality that Innocents might have is a large cranium. With their emphasis on thinking and logic to solve problems in their lives, I can see their IQs evolving to extraordinary levels over geological time. This would translate into a thicker cerebral cortex and thereby a larger brain. However, most of the increase in brain size - since many more brain structures are involved - would be due to the storage of the enormous amounts of data in the form of memories that result from the extraordinary multi-sense attention the Innocents are capable of. Over enough time, the expansion of these various parts of the Innocent's brain would cause the cranium to expand as well.

With the Innocent's emphasis on thinking and logic, what does that say about their emotions? Would they be cold emotionally? Given that Innocents (and we) are made in God's Image,[101] and God is certainly not emotionless (because we aren't), Innocents would not be emotionally cold. Instead, they would exhibit more positive emotions such as love, joy, pleasure, empathy and sympathy, and less negative emotions like fear and anxiety. There would be no anger, hate, envy, or jealously, as I have previously shown. So, Innocents would not be emotionless, but would be more positively emotional than we are. This leads to a consideration as to what their personalities would be like.

We develop our personalities through our genetics, our individual experiences, and our thoughts about those experiences.[102] In other words, we make decisions about who we are based on the cumulative personality-related information we have acquired. Comparing the personalities of the Guilty with those of the Innocent, we, the Guilty, would tend to have darker personalities, based on our more negative backgrounds, whereas Innocents with their more positive history, would have sunnier personalities. This translates into Innocents with winning personalities.

The last characteristic involves their body. Since there are no enemies to contend with, there would be no need to have big, muscular bodies for defence. Thus, the Innocent's body would evolve to slightness over time.

So, there we have it. Innocents would have large eyes, big heads, and slim bodies. Sound familiar? Assuming, of course, that Innocents are humanoid in appearance, that description sounds a lot like that of the classic space aliens that have apparently been visiting us.[103] My inference here is that these aliens are Innocents from another planet. But why have they visited us? Were they curious to see how the other half lives? Or were they just slumming it? When and if we get to meet them again, maybe we should ask.

THE WORLD
OF THE INNOCENT

I had stated at the beginning of this book that I would attempt to produce a montage of the Innocent's world that might enable us to get a general idea of what it would be like there. The world of the Innocent would be primarily a place of singularities: one race, one colour, one language, one religion, one nation, and one government. But it would also have abundance: a Tree of Life in practically every neighbourhood; land that is virtually all arable; a cornucopia of food; mountains of money; and of course, plenty of people. Finally, there are things the world of the Innocent would not have: crime, war, terrorism, drug dens, bars, big business, big pharma, pollution, and starvation. The world of the Innocent would be very different from our world.

The Innocent's phenomenal intelligence, logical ability, and caring nature are the drivers that would shape their world. People would be respectful to each other, the environment would be clean, and the air pure. Children would not be afraid of strangers because they know that no one would harm them. Food would be cheap. Charity freely given.

The world would be peaceful and quiet. No bombs going off. No gunfire. Virtually no ambulances or police cars wailing. Traffic noise would be mute partly because the internal combustion engine would be history, but also because Innocents would have perfected road surface noise reduction that we, the Guilty, have only just begun.[104] Everything would be run via the sun's energy, cars especially; boats and planes too. Aside from possible building construction, the only noise that might be heard would be the birds chirping and the occasional dog barking.

Innocents are the embodiment of sociability, so cities would tend to be crowded. But everyone would like it that way; more opportunities to party. That would also translate into more countryside to enjoy. No slums since there would be no desperately poor. No homeless or panhandlers, either.

News would be boring. It would be almost always good news: the Smith family just had triplets; new housing is being put up for the poor; a flea market is being held this weekend; a communal church membership drive has generated an ever-growing congregation; Ms. Jones is running for the President of the World, and so on. No crime and no wars to report. Hardly worth it to buy a paper.

Occasionally, however, there would be an interesting bit of news in the Science and Technology section of their newspaper. The Innocents would learn of a new planet that's been discovered where the inhabitants appear to be a lower form of life, similar to the Innocent's apes, with small heads and eyes and big bodies. But unlike their apes, they seem to have a rudimentary form of science and technology. They are warlike, though, and if they ever get to the stage where they are able to venture out into space, they would probably have exterminated themselves long before becoming a threat to the Innocents.

The Innocents would live with some dangers, but not many. Technology would be everywhere, so their lives would be ones of relative ease. Thinking, logic, and each other would be their main interests: mathematics, science, philosophy.

The world of the Innocents would be a safe place, a peaceful place, a beautiful place, a place where one can truly experience the wonder and joy of living. The future would be bright and people would be happy. And to be immortal on top of that. What could be better? Only Heaven could be better.

THE WORLD
OF THE GUILTY

I am currently living with my daughter who is in her forties and suffers from what has been diagnosed as extreme social anxiety. I think that her condition is closely connected to the fact that she was bullied in high school. She denies there is any connection, that this is who she is. She is saving up money so she can go live in the woods, free from people.

Something happened the other day that caused me to realize my daughter is emotionally stuck as a teenager. The details don't matter, only the trauma she was going through over what was a trivial situation she was facing. I stood there aghast at how she was reacting. And then it hit me: my daughter was emotionally still a teenager. I had a chance to talk to her about it later, but in the meantime, I emailed my wife and told her what I had realized about our daughter's emotional state.

When I received my wife's response, I realized we had failed our daughter. As a couple, we were so consumed with each other that we had nothing left for our daughter. I was so self-centered that I drew my wife's attention away from my daughter onto me and my troubles. Like my mother before her, coping with my father's alcoholism, my wife could only do so much, and though she did her best to raise our daughter she couldn't give her the attention she needed. It is my fault that my daughter was effectively abandoned, the one we had sworn to love and protect. It's hard to believe that love could do that, be so exclusive as to drive others away. I'm ashamed now to think how selfish I was.

Despite the distress and guilt I feel over what happened to my daughter, the analytical side of my brain began to assert itself. This situation with my daughter had a coincidence-factor that was hard to believe. My daughter went through, more or less, the same traumatization that I had experienced as a child. I was traumatized when I was very young when fostered out to strangers multiple times. After returning home, I was further traumatized when my parents ignored my cries for attention and comfort. How can that happen, two successive generations going through highly similar trauma? My daughter did not need to be bullied in school. She could have been spared. Then she wouldn't have experienced the parental neglect we gave her.

Our family is not unique in this. Families tend to pass down their trauma. Studies have shown that similar trauma is experienced inter-generationally.[105] In that sense, family trees can be viewed as trauma pathways, with each generation experiencing similar levels of suffering. Thus, it may be supposed that each family tree can be identified by it's particular level of suffering, wherein the level of suffering becomes predictable, generation to generation.

Not every individual is able to endure the same level of suffering. So, family trees having identifiable trauma pathways suggests God uses that fact in assigning individuals to their next lives. Since God believes in free choice, these individuals must have input into what level of suffering they are willing to endure. From this, God would determine which family tree best suits that choice. The more suffering they can endure, the closer to God they will be, and the relevant family tree they will be assigned to. That also suggests members of certain family trees are inherently closer to God than others.

This puts a whole new complexion on how we live our lives on this planet. What happens to us here, in terms of our suffering, is both deliberate and random. Deliberate because we chose this life and the amount of suffering it has in store for us, and random in that we don't know exactly what kind of suffering is going to hit us and when. The only thing that is certain is that God will make sure we suffer no more than we have agreed to.

The only conclusion left is that what happens to us - that our suffering is not wholly random - is that God has been managing a scenario for us so we can suffer, but in a controlled way. You've heard the phrase: "The devil's in the details"? Well, for us and our lives, God is definitely into the details. He will not let us suffer more than we think we can take.

This all suggests that God, in His Infinite Wisdom, knows what is going to happen to us in any life we choose. How does He know this? Besides being God, that is? I think the only way He can know what is going to happen to us is if He has already gone through it Himself, that He has in fact lived innumerable lives and suffered immeasurably. He doesn't look into His crystal ball and predict what is going to happen to us in the future; He already knows. Sounds like a masochist to me. Either that or our God seeks to truly be The One, The Only, All Powerful, and All Knowing God. Personally, I choose the latter. I wouldn't want to offend a god like that. I didn't realize He was so ambitious, though.

You, the reader, may not agree with my reasoning regarding our willingness to endure the suffering of losing a child simply so that we could someday find ourselves in God's Presence. If you think that, you need to ask yourself this question: What is the point to the suffering we endure on this planet? Is it so that we can go to Heaven? Properly regulated (which is what God is doing for us), suffering can build strength of character. If you think that going to Heaven is the reward for the suffering we endure here on Earth, then what do we need the strength of character that comes from that suffering? Strength of character is primarily needed for one thing: psychological endurance, and you don't need that in Heaven.[106] There is only one place you would need the kind of endurance that comes from a strong character acquired from multiple lives of suffering, and that is in the Presence of the Raw Power and Glory of Almighty God. We are all here in a quest to build the kind of character that will enable us to enter into God's Inner Sanctum.

Indeed, what you, the reader, think now, the decisions you have made during this life, may not have anything to do with your original decision to eat the fruit of the Tree of the Knowledge of Good and Evil and your subsequent choice regarding the level of suffering you were willing to endure. Before you entered this life, you might even have chosen the highest level of suffering a human can take, whatever you think that is. And that means that you judge your character to be strong enough to be able to make such a choice. That also means that you must have had a deep love of God and an urgency to be with Him, despite what you may think now. That person, the one who made that choice, is the person you truly are.

What if you commit evil? You too, by the fact that you are here among us, must have shared our desire to be with God when you entered this life. How does committing evil affect your place on the way to God? Logic dictates that for every act of suffering you commit, you must move further away from God - not to mention facilitating your victim's move closer to Him. This means too, that in order to again move closer to God, you must recover lost ground by repeating the previous suffering you had already endured. In a sense, it's true: by hurting someone else, inevitably you hurt yourself.

Suffering has the capacity to do one of two things: build strong character or destroy it. If you can benefit from your suffering by building strong character, you will become closer to God. However, if you can't, you will destroy character, in which case, you will move away from God. Instead of becoming more like God, you become more like the devil. This can even result in evil behaviour: you may now want to inflict suffering, rather than endure it.

How does one actually build strong character amid suffering? We know the saying. "What doesn't kill you, makes you stronger". But it doesn't tell you how to get that strength. Basically it says that if you can endure the suffering without committing suicide, you should be stronger. It should not be just a matter of figuratively gritting your teeth, hoping you will come out stronger in the end. There has to be a process, a middle step, that one must take in order to achieve strong character. From personal experience, I call that step "Gaining Wisdom".

Some time ago, I found myself instrumental in putting a young dog to sleep. The dog was not mine, it was my daughter's, but I had grown to love it as my own.

Unfortunately, the dog - Eddie was his name - had a genetic abnormality that caused the bones of his spine to squeeze the spinal cord, eventually damaging it to the point where he could not use his hind legs. He was paralyzed.

Rather than letting him continue to suffer, my daughter decided to put him to sleep. I agreed. However, when she described the scene at the vet's, how Eddie was so happy to see her among these strangers, only to be betrayed by putting him to sleep, it broke my heart, as it did her.

For months I couldn't get over that picture of Eddie being so happy, only to be put down. Finally, I asked Jesus to help me. He sent this message: "One cannot truly love unless one is willing to fully experience the loss of that love." Somehow, I felt relieved. After that, I was able to think of Eddie without breaking down. I still love him, but not with the pain I once felt. I had gained some wisdom and I think my character grew that day. I pray that you, the reader, will accept the wisdom of Jesus into your life.

How does our world, the world of the Guilty, compare to that of the Innocents? How far from God's mark have we fallen? That question can probably best be answered about how well or poorly we are doing as a species by how close we feel we are to our own destruction. We have a clock for that. It's called, appropriately, the Doomsday Clock. How many minutes we judge ourselves to be before midnight, the symbolic indicator of our imminent demise, represents how close we feel we are to our own destruction. At the time of this writing, we are at 90 seconds to midnight. That is pretty close. In fact, over the past decade we have been trending closer to this symbolic time of self-destruction.[107]

Whether the Doomsday Clock and the time set on it represents our fate remains to be seen. However, it can't be denied that we are in some serious trouble when it comes to our survival on this planet: hostile nations with nuclear weapons; an upsurge in terrorism that has the potential to go nuclear; global warming which could change the face of our planet; environmental degradation that threatens our food supply, just to name a few. The Innocent's world would be nowhere near our state of failure in adherence to God's principles. So, I can safely say, without fear of contradiction from the Innocents, that they are probably praying for us right now somewhere in the universe.

I'm thinking of my life in this world of the Guilty and how I eventually came to Jesus to ask Him to take over the reins. I began to notice a change in me from that point on. I became more caring, more thoughtful of others, abhorred violence, and even went back to church. The softening of my attitude towards others was the most noticeable change in me since being Saved by Jesus.[108] I also realized what I was before

I met Jesus. I was less caring, more selfish, more violent, and less sympathetic to the suffering of others. I didn't like who I had been. It is my prayer that you, the reader, would also experience the Salvation that is Jesus Christ.

During the writing of this book, a song popped into my head. It was a song written by the Rolling Stones back in the sixties called "A Heart of Stone". At first, I didn't know why it was there. It was just 'rolling' around in my head, over and over. Slowly, I began to make a connection between what I was writing in this book and what the song represented.

The song "A Heart of Stone" is the story of how a man was abusing the love of women. This man was warning a particular girl who was walking down the street towards him to carry on walking and to not stop, for he had no love in him, that he enjoyed making girls cry.

"He had no love in him." What does that mean? Did he not love women at all? If he didn't, then how did he feel about the rest of humanity? I'm sure the writer of this song didn't intend for that statement to be taken literally, but the fact that it was popularized into a song suggests that this behaviour was in some way acceptable, that it was okay to hurt people, and even enjoy it. I am wary of people who think that way.

Now that I am Saved, I find it difficult to watch violent movies. I suddenly have a deep empathy for the innocent people who were hurt or killed, even though I know it is all make believe. For me, it has become very real.

I had taken a step back towards being more human, that is, more caring. I didn't even suspect I was not as caring until I was Saved. It causes me to think that those who are not Saved are also less caring, less human than they would be otherwise. Is that the road we are on, becoming less human towards each other? Will we end up as psychopaths with no compassion for each other, if we continue down that road? Will we lose the capacity to fall in love?[109] Are we all developing hearts of stone?

I know that we live in a violent world where there are people only too willing to attack, injure, and even kill us. To be the recipients of such violence is noble, it will get you further up the road to everlasting peace with God. To inflict it is cowardly. You succumb to your own hate.

There are two types of suffering in this world that will get you closer to God. There is the self-sacrificial kind, the kind where you stand up for another, you take the pain they would have if you hadn't been willing to take their place. This is the kind of suffering Jesus went through for us. The other kind is the suffering of a victim. This kind of suffering could be from an accident, disease, or a malicious act, it doesn't matter. It only matters how you endure and deal with these two types of suffering that will indicate where on the road to God you will find yourself.

We have been at war for almost all of our recorded history, some 3,400 years. We've only found peace for 268 years or

8% of that time.[110] In relative terms, those few peaceful years are a measure of how generally ineffective we have been in using logic to settle our disputes, if we used logic at all. I'm sure that disputes had arisen during those peaceful periods, we just decided not to kill each other for a change and instead settled those disputes amicably. It's too bad we couldn't have done it more often; we might not be in the kind of serious trouble we find ourselves currently in our world, had we done so.

Some would argue that sometimes you have to go to war, that it's, in a way, logical. But is war logical? Given that we are here for a purpose, to be with Almighty God, and that we must suffer to do so, then how does war facilitate that? On both sides there is suffering, not only for the soldiers, but for the civilians as well. That suffering surely will get the victims closer to God. But what about those who inflict that suffering? I've stated previously that those who commit evil – and killing is surely evil, whether or not it is sanctioned by the government - must ultimately lose in their struggle to be with God. First, they lose because their actions cause them to move further away from God. Second, they lose by having to re-experience previous suffering they had already endured when they once again begin moving closer to God. Also, in a sense, they lose a third time by enabling those they harm to possibly move ahead of them in their own quest to be with God. So, from those points of view, war is a losing proposition, no matter who ostensibly wins. Ironically, the only ones who ultimately win a war are the victims.

We've had plenty of time to turn things around and get our behaviour right towards each other, but we chose the easy way, to succumb to our hate and spite, just to even the score. The other side, however, takes that as their cue, to retaliate, and in the process, up the stakes. Now, we've reached the nuclear bomb stage of our weapons development, where we can wipe each other out in one grand orgasm of self-destruction.

Of course, we don't really want this. We are supposedly rational, thinking human beings, who want nothing more than to live in peace with one another. Is it too late to turn things around? We thought that with the nuclear bomb in our arsenal we had reached the MAD stage (Mutual Assured Destruction) where no one would be crazy enough to actually push the button that would send us all to oblivion.[111] However, in light of recent events: U.S. President Donald J. Trump's erratic behaviour; North Korea's dictator, Kim Jung Un's nuclear program and missile provocations, and now with Putin's threat to go nuclear in his war with Ukraine, we're not so sure anymore.[112][113] At 90 seconds to midnight on our Doomsday Clock, we know that despite having been at this clock position before, the minute hand will probably be moving even closer. So it is time to act if we want to reverse its direction.

My focus has been to use deductive logic in this book, which means the conclusions reached must be true, if the premises are true. You will see a list of the major conclusions that were reached in this book in the next chapter. Logic is a useful tool that can provide solutions that would otherwise escape us. It is now time for logic to rule our behaviour on this planet, so that we may avoid transforming it and ourselves into a burning ball of destruction and death.

I beseech all of us to change our path, to choose a different way, one that is firmly based in the logical ability that God, and Jesus, gave to us all.

You have now read the main body of this book and should be able to make an informed choice when answering the question "Which life would you choose?" presented at the beginning of this book. It should be obvious now that you were being offered a choice between living in an Innocent world or living in a Guilty world. You also know that upon entering this life, you chose the second option, a life of suffering.

I'll leave you with a final question: Which option will you choose for your NEXT life?

CONCLUSIONS

I think we've seen that logic can achieve some remarkable results. This chapter will list the major conclusions that were reached in this book.

1. The first beings, Adam and Eve, were not created immortal.
2. Being sinless does not guarantee immortality.
3. The Tree of Life is not a Tree that gives immortal life, but a life sustainer, maintaining the human body indefinitely.
4. Adam, Eve, and the Innocents, needed to periodically eat the fruit of the Tree of Life in order to be effectively immortal.
5. God has felt like committing evil.
6. Evil does not originate in us. It comes from the Tree of the Knowledge of Good and Evil.

7. If Innocents, being immortal, allowed themselves to populate their world at an indiscriminate rate, they could overpopulate it in less than 625 years.

8. Innocents would experience many of the same negative emotions we feel, such as fear, frustration, anxiety, and worry. However, they would not feel anger, hate, jealously, or envy. They can be traumatized though, but not for long.

9. Innocent bodies would be in perfect running order, with perfect eyesight and hearing. They would also have excellent memories and incredibly high IQs.

10. The Innocents would have large eyes, big heads, and slim bodies.

11. The Innocent's world would have no crime, no war, no pollution, and no starvation. Also, Innocents would be practically disease free.

12. We are not alone in the universe. In fact, the other occupants of our universe are just alien versions of the Innocent and the Guilty.

13. God did not forbid Adam and Eve from eating the fruit of the Tree of the Knowledge of Good and Evil, He warned them. The biblical story of Adam and Eve in the Garden of Eden is actually about choice, a choice of how you want live your life. The Tree of Life and the Tree of the Knowledge of Good and Evil represent the choices. Choosing the Tree of Life brings

you an immortal life of happiness and contentment. Choosing the Tree of the Knowledge of Good and Evil will get you a mortal life of suffering, sometimes great suffering, more than can be imagined; but all for the right to stand in the Magnificent but Terrible Presence of Almighty God.

14. We have lived past lives.

15. God has lived innumerable lives and suffered immeasurably. This is how He became Almighty God.

16. God is directing our lives in order to ensure that we don't suffer more than we think we can bear. He is doing this so we can someday be with Him.

17. The more suffering we can take, the closer we will be to Almighty God.

18. We are here to suffer in order to build the strength of character necessary to enable us to enter into God's Inner Sanctum.

19. Why does a benevolent God allow suffering in the world? The answer is because we chose the level of suffering we would endure before we entered this life, so it should be no surprise that we suffer. God is simply honouring an agreement that we made. And just as Jesus suffered in order that He might ascend to the right hand of God, we are doing much the same thing.[114]

POSTFACE

My approach to writing this book was to be logical, but within a religious context. In the process, however, I made God knowable. He grew into the job of being God, that is, He wasn't always God, for He once (or more often) felt like committing evil. Whether He actually did commit evil, I don't know. He is also ambitious, he wanted to be The One, The Only, All Powerful, All Knowing God of the Universe. In other words, God started out much like any of us. Which opens up the possibility as to what any of us ultimately could be.

God doesn't always answer prayers, and I think for a reason. The person chooses the amount of suffering s/he is willing to endure, but when actually confronted with that suffering, wants to avoid it. Thus, the praying. However, if God sees that they agreed to this amount of suffering, He will not answer their prayer. Hopefully, they will thank Him in the end.

It has taken me 7 years to write this book. During that time, I've tried to imagine a truly Innocent world. Unfortunately, in the process, I've come to realize just how evil our world is: assaults, sexual and otherwise, murders, child abuse, bombings, torture, terrorism, wars, robbery, muggings, mass shootings, extortion, kidnapping, corruption, pollution, starvation, homelessness, adultery, slander, libel, and of course, ubiquitous lying, just to name some of the evil we get up to. Any Innocent alien visiting our world for the first time might consider it a truly mad place. How can people do these things to each other if they were not insane? Would the Innocent aliens even dare to contact us? Being born into this insanity might make it seem somehow normal. But we know, in the back of our minds, that it's not. Insanity aside, there is one more thing that would dissuade the Innocents from openly contacting us: they have the Tree of Life, something we, the Guilty, should NEVER have.

Ours is a world that needs major corrections. Consider: what if we could make one correction that would somehow take care of the rest, even global warming? What would that correction need to be? The common characteristic of all actions in the world that critically need correcting are those that cause harm - directly or indirectly - to human beings. All other actions don't cry out for correction, only those that harm us. So, adopting a regimen wherein not causing harm to another is promoted, could have added benefits. Especially when considering that we wouldn't need to focus our efforts on correcting a wide range of behaviours; we just have to focus on one: doing no harm to another. As long as we keep it in mind to perform no action that could conceivably harm another, then all other negative actions should eventually be corrected.

How do we change our thoughts and behaviour? Normally, by first changing our behaviour. Eventually, our thoughts will change as well. A kind of "fake it, 'til you make it" approach.

If you are a Christian, however, the hard work is already being done for you. Jesus is working within you to change your thoughts by creating a New You in His image. In the process, your behaviour changes as well.

How does one build strong character? One way, is by becoming more innocent. This is what is happening to me. Over the 7 years that I have been working on this book, my thoughts and behaviour have become more innocent. What I mean by that is, one, I am more abhorrent of violence, and two, I feel another's pain and suffering more deeply. I don't even kill spiders anymore, because of the time I threw one into a flushing toilet and I saw how it desperately tried to escape. My heart went out to it and I instantly regretted what I had done. Seems silly, doesn't it? Not to me anymore. I've gone from the self-centered narcissist I once was to something of an empath. I feel a deep empathy for those who suffer as I've never felt before. At times, it's painful. It's those times that I pray to Jesus to help me endure. In short, I've become more human. Of course, I have been reading my book over and over, and this has helped to focus my thoughts in the proper direction. It's a form of end-goal visualization.

Doesn't it seem contradictory that having strong character should make one seem like an emotional pushover? It's not really all that surprising considering that among the attributes of strong character are empathy and compassion. So, though I may seem like an emotional marshmallow, my capacity to emotionally suffer has increased. [115]

Here is another thought to consider: We have been suffering for as long as we have existed here on Earth. In fact, in many arenas of our existence the scale of our suffering has increased: atomic bomb attacks, national starvation, the refugee crisis, genocide, pandemics, etc. Even our weather is causing us more misery.

At the same time, in our progress further up the path to God, the closer we get to God, the more suffering we choose to endure. Question: Could the suffering we experience here on Earth be merely a reflection of our journey to be closer to God? Is it coincidental or causal?

Could we subconsciously be manipulating world events, and even our individual lives, to match the progress of our suffering in our mission to be with God? If true, it suggests that things will only get worse here on Earth. That poses other questions: How much worse will it get before we finally arrive at the Godhead? Will it be necessary to bring ourselves to the brink of a world war, or even war itself, in order to have suffered enough to qualify for the Godhead? Will we destroy ourselves and leave Earth a wasteland before we do? What has to change in order to avoid that outcome?

We could change our behaviour by becoming more innocent. Although our suffering will temporarily increase because we no longer have the revenge outlet to mitigate our misery, we may have escaped our own destruction. This increase in suffering could even be enough for us to qualify for the Godhead.[116]

The point is that as long as we yearn to be with God, and continue choosing more suffering in order to accomplish that, we may come to a crossroads where we must choose between innocence or annihilation.

There is another choice you can make to help endure the suffering of the Guilty world's possible end: ask for the help of Jesus Christ by making Him your Lord and Saviour. I pray that you make that choice, before it's too late.

REFERENCES

NKJV scripture taken from the New King James Version Bible. Copyright © 1979, 1980, 1982 by Thomas Nelson, Inc. Used with permission. All rights reserved.

WIL scripture taken from the Word in Life™ Contemporary English Version (CEV) Bible. Copyright © 1993, 1996, 1998 by Thomas Nelson, Inc. Used with permission.

Quran scripture taken from the Quran English Translation. Translated by Talal Itani. Published by ClearQuran, Dallas, Beirut. Provided under terms of the Creative Commons License.

[1]   NKJV Bible. Job ch 14 vs 1-4, Psalms ch 51 vs 5, ch 58 vs 3, Proverbs ch 22 vs 15, Romans ch 3 vs 23
       Wellman, J. What Christians Want to Know. (n.d.) "Why are we born sinners? A Bible Study" Retrieved from https://www.whatchristianswanttoknow.com/why-are-we-born-sinners-a-bible-study/

[2]   Bradford, A. Live Science (2017) "Deductive Reasoning vs Inductive Reasoning" Retrieved from https://www.livescience.com/21569-deduction-vs-induction.html

[3]   NKJV Bible. Genesis ch 2 vs 15 – 25, ch 3 vs 1 – 24

[4]   Railsback, B. University of Georgia Department of Geology. (2000) *Creation Stories from around the World* (#14. Yahweh) Retrieved from http://railsback.org/CS/CSIndex.html

[5]   NKJV Bible. Exodus ch 19 vs 10 - 24, ch 33 vs 17 - 23

[6]   NKJV Bible. Genesis ch 2 vs 17, ch 5 - 11

[7]   WIL (CEV) Bible. Romans ch 5 vs 12

[8]   NKJV Bible. Genesis ch 3 vs 22 - 24
       Alcorn, R. Eternal Perspective Ministries (2016) "What is the Tree of Life?" Retrieved from https://www.crosswalk.com/faith/bible-study/what-is-the-tree-of-life.html
       Editorial Staff. Christianity.com (2021) "What is the Tree of Life? Biblical Meaning and Importance" Retrieved from https://www.christianity.com/wiki/christian-terms/tree-of-life-bible-meaning.html
       International Standard Bible Encyclopedia (n.d.) "Tree of Life" Retrieved from https://www.biblestudytools.com/encyclopedias/isbe/tree-of-life.html

[9]   Nicholas, D. The Tablet. (2017) "Natural Disasters Are Part of Original Sin" Retrieved from https://thetablet.org/natural-disasters-are-part-of-original-sin/
       Rodriguez, A. M. Biblical Research Institute. (2018) "Are Natural Disasters God's Punishment?" Retrieved from https://www.adventistbiblicalresearch.org/materials/theology-judgment/are-natural-disasters-gods-punishment

[10] Kleiman, K. Cities Church (2018) "The Suffering of Jesus"
Retrieved from https://www.citieschurch.com/sermons/
the-suffering-of-jesus
      Church of the Great God (n.d.) "Bible Verses About Jesus
Christ's Suffering" Retrieved from https://www.cgg.org/index.
cfm/library/verses/id/2992/jesus-christs-suffering-verses.htm
      Real Presence Eucharistic Education and Adoration
Association (n.d) "The Apostles' Creed" Retrieved from http://
www.therealpresence.org/essentials/creed/acc07.htm

[11] WIL (CEV) Bible. Job ch 23 vs 10, 1 Peter ch 1 vs 7,
Zechariah ch 13 vs 9, Proverbs ch 17 vs 3, Psalms ch 66 vs 10,
James ch 1 vs 12, Isaiah ch 48 vs 10, 1 Peter ch 1 vs 6-7, Psalm ch 66 vs 10-12,
1 Peter ch 4 vs 12-13, Malachi ch 3 vs 3, 1 Peter ch 5 vs 10, Isaiah ch 1 vs 25,
James ch 1 vs 2-4, Jeremiah ch 9 vs 7, Proverbs ch 2 vs 4, Psalm ch 17 vs 3,
2 Thessalonians ch 1 vs 7, James ch 1 vs 3, Proverbs ch 27 vs 21, 1 Peter ch 4 vs 1,
Deuteronomy ch 8 vs 2, Revelation ch 3 vs 10, 2 Timothy ch 3 vs 12, Romans
ch 5 vs 3-4, Revelation ch 7 vs 14, Revelation ch 2 vs 10, 1 Peter ch 1 vs 7-8,
Lamentations ch 3 vs 1-66, Romans ch 5 vs 3 Proverbs 17:3, Psalm 66:10,
1 Peter 4:12-13.

[12] WIL (CEV) Bible. Exodus ch 20 vs 3-17

[13] Food and Agriculture Organization of the United Nations. (2011)
[pdf] *Labour* Retrieved from http://www.fao.org/3/i2490e/
i2490e01b.pdf
      Chait, J. thebalancesmallbusiness (2019) "What is the
Definition of an Agricultural Product?" Retrieved from https://
www.thebalancesmb.com/what-is-an-agricultural-product-2538211
      Study Read (n.d.) "Why is Agriculture Important | Its Role
in Everyday Life" Retrieved from https://www.studyread.com/
importance-of-agriculture/

[14] Pollock, J. MIT (Massachusetts Institute of Technology)
Technological Review. (2007) "Green Revolutionary"
Retrieved from https://www.technologyreview.com/s/409243/
green-revolutionary/
      Myers, N. Current Science. (1999) [pdf] *The next green
revolution: its environmental underpinnings* Retrieved from https://
www.jstor.org/stable/24100752?seq=1

[15]   Hunger Notes. (2018) World Hunger and Poverty
Facts and Statistics. *Number of Hungry People in the
World*. Retrieved from https://www.worldhunger.org/
world-hunger-and-poverty-facts-and-statistics/

[16]   Food and Agriculture Organization of the United Nations. (n.d.)
What effect will biofuels have on forest land and poor people's access to it?
Retrieved from www.fao.org/docrep/011/i0440e/i0440e07.htm

[17]   Paperny, A.M. Global News Network. (2015) "Going Hungry: Why
millions of Canadians can't afford healthy food" Retrieved from
http://globalnews.ca/news/1903255/going-hungry-why-millions-of-
canadians-cant-afford-healthy-food/

[18]   Parks, J. Live Science. (2014) "Soil-free farming grows vegetables
in the desert" Retrieved from https://www.livescience.com/42835-
soil-free-farming-grows-vegetables-in-the-desert.html
     Meagan. American Museum of Natural History. (2015)
*Superabsorbant Hydrogels: A Study of the Most Effective Application
of Cross-linked Polyacrylamide Polymers* Retrieved from
https://www.amnh.org/learn-teach/curriculum-collections/
young-naturalist-awards/winning-essays/2009/superabsorbant-
hydrogels-a-study-of-the-most-effective-application-of-cross-
linked-polyacrylamide-polymers

[19]   PG Economics. (2014) *GM crop use continue to
benefit the environment and farmers* Retrieved from
https://pgeconomics.co.uk/press+releases/5/GM+crop+use+
continues+to+benefit+the+environment+and+farmers
     Medlineplus. (n.d.)"Genetically Engineered Foods" Retrieved
from https://medlineplus.gov/ency/article/002432.htm

[20]   Wilkerson, J. Harvard University. (2015) *Why Roundup Ready Crops
Have Lost Their Allure* Retrieved from http://sitn.hms.harvard.edu/
flash/2015/roundup-ready-crops/
     Dasgupta, S. Mongabay (2016) "How many plant species
are there in the world? Scientists now have an answer"
Retrieved from https://news.mongabay.com/2016/05/
many-plants-world-scientists-may-now-answer/

[21] Food and Agriculture Organization of the United Nations. (2014) *Arable Land (% of Land Area)* Retrieved from data.worldbank.org/indicator/AG.LND.ARBL.ZS

[22] Lederer, E.M. Global News Network. (2017) "20 million people in 4 countries facing starvation, famine: UN" Retrieved from http://globalnews.ca/news/3303014/20-million-people-in-4-countries-facing-starvation-famine-u-n/

[23] CBC News. (2011) "Somalia food aid stolen, sold in markets" Retrieved from http://www.cbc.ca/news/world/somalia-food-aid-stolen-sold-in-markets-1.1033052

[24] Bacon, D. Political Research Associates. (2014) *Globalization and NAFTA Caused Migration from Mexico.* Retrieved from https://politicalresearch.org/2014/10/11/globalization-and-nafta-caused-migration-from-mexico
U.S Library of Congress (n.d.) Immigration and Relocation in U.S. History Retrieved from https://www.loc.gov/classroom-materials/immigration/mexican/expansion-and-expulsion/

[25] Shirley, A. World Economic Forum. (2016) "Which are the world's most polluted cities?" Retrieved from https://www.weforum.org/agenda/2016/05/which-are-the-world-s-most-polluted-cities/

[26] MyHealthPortal. (2010) "The health effects of air pollution in Hong Kong" Retrieved from https://web.archive.org/web/20140630141739/http://www.myhealthportal.hk/en/content/articles/18/Health_Effects_of_Air_Pollution_in_Hong_Kong/

[27] Sparks, M. New Scientist. (2022) "Chernobyl power cut sparks fears of potential for radiation leaks" Retrieved from https://www.newscientist.com/article/2311591-chernobyl-power-cut-sparks-fears-of-potential-for-radiation-leaks/
Glantz, M. United States Institute of Peace. (2022) "Russia's New Nuclear Threat: Power Plants as Weapons" Retrieved from https://www.usip.org/publications/2022/08/russias-new-nuclear-threat-power-plants-weapons

[28] World Nuclear Association. (2016) *Chernobyl Accident 1986*
Retrieved from http://world-nuclear.org/information-library/
safety-and-security/safety-of-plants/chernobyl-accident.aspx
Pleasance, C. Mail Online News. (2015) "Living And Working
In Chernobyl: Fascinating Insight Into The Lives Of Those Who
Work And Live In The Exclusion Zone Around The Nuclear Plant
Nearly 30 Years After Disaster That Shook The World" Retrieved
from http://www.dailymail.co.uk/news/article-3019536/Living-
working-Chernobyl-Fascinating-insight-lives-work-live-exclusion-
zone-nuclear-plant-nearly-30-years-disaster-shook-world.html

[29] Jacobson, M.Z., Ten Hoeve, J.E. Earth & Environmental Science.
(2012) *Worldwide health effects of the Fukushima Daiichi nuclear
accident.* Retrieved from https://web.stanford.edu/group/efmh/
jacobson/TenHoeveEES12.pdf
World Nuclear Association. (2017) *Fukushima
Accident* Retrieved from http://www.world-nuclear.org/
information-library/safety-and-security/safety-of-plants/
fukushima-accident.aspx
Holt, M. Campbell, R. J. Nikitin, M. B. Federation of American
Scientists/Congressional Research Service Report. (2012) [pdf]
Fukushima Nuclear Accident Retrieved from https://fas.org/sgp/
crs/nuke/R41694.pdf

[30] Marks, K. Soap Boxie (2019) "How Bad is Water Pollution in
America?" Retrieved from https://soapboxie.com/social-issues/
How-Bad-Is-Water-Pollution-in-America
Saier, M.H., Trevers, J.T. U.S. National Library of Science
(2009) *Global Pollution: How Much Is Too Much?* Retrieved from
https://www.ncbi.nlm.nih.gov/pmc/articles/PMC3229874/

[31] ListAKA. (n.d.) "12 Most Polluted Rivers in the World" Retrieved
from listaka.com/top-12-most-polluted-rivers-in-the-world
Kibria, G. Royal Melbourne Institute of Technology
University. (2016) *World Rivers in Crisis: Water Quality and Water
Biodiversity are at Risk* Retrieved from https://www.researchgate.
net/publication/310054582_World_rivers_in_crisis_water_
quality_and_water_dependent_biodiversity_are_at_risk-_
Threats_of_pollution_climate_change_dam%27s_development

[32] Mosley, S. Leeds Metropolitan University. (n.d.) *Environmental History of Air Pollution and Protection* Retrieved from http://www.eolss.net/sample-chapters/c09/e6-156-15.pdf

Weebly.com. (n.d.) "The Industrial Revolution: Working and Living Conditions" Retrieved from http://firstindustrialrevolution.weebly.com/working-and-living-conditions.html

Aldrich, M. Economic History Association. (2001) *History of Workplace Safety in the United States, 1880-1970.* Retrieved from http://eh.net/encyclopedia/history-of-workplace-safety-in-the-united-states-1880-1970/

[33] Suskind, R. U.S. National Library of Medicine, National Institute of Medicine (1977) *Environmental Health Perspective: Environment and the Skin* Retrieved from https://www.ncbi.nlm.nih.gov/pmc/articles/PMC1637330/

Leen, S. National Geographic, n.d. "Human Skin Color Variation" Retrieved from https://humanorigins.si.edu/evidence/genetics/human-skin-color-variation

World Health Organization, "Radiation: Ultraviolet (UV) Radiation (2016) Retrieved from https://www.who.int/news-room/questions-and-answers/item/radiation-ultraviolet-(uv)

[34] NKJV Bible. Genesis ch 11 vs 1-9

[35] National Geographic Society. (2013) "Global Human Journey" Retrieved from https://www.nationalgeographic.org/media/global-human-journey/

[36] Boundless Biology. Libretexts (2019) *The Galapagos Finches and Natural Selection* Retrieved from https://bio.libretexts.org/Bookshelves/Introductory_and_General_Biology/Book%3A_General_Biology_(Boundless)/18%3A_Evolution_and_the_Origin_of_Species/18.1%3A_Understanding_Evolution/18.1C%3A_The_Galapagos_Finches_and_Natural_Selection

[37] Gray, A.W. et al. Encyclopaedia Britannica (2020) "Origins of Agriculture" Retrieved from https://www.britannica.com/topic/agriculture

[38] National Geographic Society. (n.d.) "Border" Retrieved from
https://www.nationalgeographic.org/encyclopedia/border/

[39] Reference (n.d.) "What are the Four Main Purposes of
Government?" Retrieved from https://www.reference.com/
world-view/four-main-purposes-government-b6434dfd838c05a0

[40] Your US-Brazil Trade Assist. (2017) "Regional Trade
Blocks, Tariffs and Trade Barriers" Retrieved from
http://www.rosalienebacchus.com/articles/
RegionalTradeBlocks.html
      Economics Online (n.d.) "Trading Blocs" Retrieved from
https://www.economicsonline.co.uk/Global_economics/
Trading_blocs.html
      Sherman, F. bizfluent (2019) "What are the benefits of trade bloc
agreements?" Retrieved from https://bizfluent.com/facts-6311951-
benefits-trade-bloc-agreements-.html

[41] All About Philosophy. (2002) "Communism" Retrieved from http://
www.allaboutphilosophy.org/communism.htm

[42] Luders, E., Narr, K., Thompson, P.M., Toga, A.W. U.S. National
Library of Medicine, National Center for Biotechnology
Information. (2009) *Neuroanatomical Correlates of Intelligence*
Retrieved from https://www.ncbi.nlm.nih.gov/pmc/articles/
PMC2770698/

[43] Dionne Jr. E.J. The Washington Post (2012) "Two-paycheck couples
are quickly becoming the norm" Retrieved from https://www.
washingtonpost.com/opinions/two-paycheck-couples-are-quickly-
becoming-the-norm/2012/04/18/gIQALSzlRT_story.html

[44] Doughty, S. Daily Mail (2008) "Broken home children are 'five times
more likely to suffer mental troubles'" Retrieved from https://www.
dailymail.co.uk/news/article-1079510/Children-broken-homes-
times-likely-suffer-mental-troubles-says-Government-study.html
      United Families International. (n.d.) *Fatherlessness, Poverty,
and Crime* Retrieved from https://www.unitedfamilies.org/
child-development/fatherlessness-poverty-and-crime/

Ahmad Jazuli, et al. Atlantis Press. (2021) "Does Broken-Home Family Contribute to Drugs Abuse in Correctional the Most?" Retrieved from https://www.atlantis-press.com/proceedings/iclhr-20/125956222#:~:text=The%20attention%20of%20parents%20and,uncomfortable%20conditions%20in%20the%20house.

[45] NKJV Bible. Genesis ch 1 vs 28 - 31

[46] Salahi, L. ABCNews. (2011) "Study: Schoolyard Bullies Four Times More Likely To Abuse Spouses As Adults" Retrieved from https://abcnews.go.com/Health/Wellness/school-bullies-linked-domestic-violence-adults/story?id=13774706

[47] Ritchie H., Roser M. Our World in Data. (2024) "Alcohol Consumption" Retrieved from https://ourworldindata.org/alcohol-consumption
Nelson, S.C. Huffington Post UK. (2014) "World's Heaviest Drinking Countries Revealed" Retrieved from https://www.huffingtonpost.co.uk/2014/05/13/worlds-heaviest-drinking-countries-revealed-infographic_n_5314613.html

[48] United Nations Office on Drugs and Crime. World Drug Report. (2011) *Consumption: Opiates* (p. 210) [pdf] Retrieved from http://www.unodc.org/documents/data-and-analysis/WDR2011/StatAnnex-consumption.pdf

[49] U.S. Department of Health and Human Science. Prescription Drug Abuse Report. (2013) *Addressing Prescription Drug Abuse in the United States* (p. 10) [pdf] Retrieved from https://www.cdc.gov/drugoverdose/pdf/hhs_prescription_drug_abuse_report_09.2013.pdf

[50] United Nations Office on Drugs and Crime. World Drug Report. (2011) *Consumption: Cannabis* (p. 175) Retrieved from https://www.unodc.org/documents/data-and-analysis/WDR2011/World_Drug_Report_2011_ebook.pdf

[51] Heshmat, S. Ph.D. Psychology Today (2017) "Why do people drink?" Retrieved from https://www.psychologytoday.com/us/blog/science-choice/201703/why-do-people-drink

[52] Editorial Staff. American Addiction Centers (2020) "Alcoholism is a Threefold Disease" Retrieved from https://alcoholrehab.com/alcoholism/alcoholism-is-a-threefold-disease/
Buddy, T. VeryWellMind (2020) "Recognizing Alcoholism as a Disease" Retrieved from https://www.verywellmind.com/alcoholism-as-a-disease-63292

[53] Casa Palmera. (2013) "The History of Illegal Drugs in America" Retrieved from https://casapalmera.com/blog/the-history-of-illegal-drugs-in-america/

[54] National Institute on Drug Addiction. (n.d.) "Drug Misuse and Addiction" Retrieved from https://nida.nih.gov/publications/drugs-brains-behavior-science-addiction/drug-misuse-addiction

[55] MacKenbach, J.P. Journal of Epidemiology & Community Heath. (2006) *The Origins of Human Disease: a short story on "where diseases come from."* Retrieved from https://www.ncbi.nlm.nih.gov/pmc/articles/PMC2465528/

[56] Eccleston, C., Keogh, E., Moore, D.J. US National Library of Medicine, National Institute of Health. (2011) *The interruptive effect of pain on attention.* Retrieved from https://www.researchgate.net/publication/51848881_The_interruptive_effect_of_pain_on_attention

[57] Fogel, A. Psychology Today. (2012) "Emotional and Physical Pain Activate Similar Brain Regions" Retrieved from https://www.psychologytoday.com/blog/body-sense/201204/emotional-and-physical-pain-activate-similar-brain-regions

[58] Winch, G. Psychology Today. (2014) "10 Things You Didn't Know About Guilt" Retrieved from https://www.psychologytoday.com/blog/the-squeaky-wheel/201411/10-things-you-didnt-know-about-guilt

[59] Meier, S. Psyc 372 University of Idaho. Physiological Psychology. (n.d.) [pdf] *Brain Structures That Are Involved With Memory.* (p. 23) Retrieved from https://webpages.uidaho.edu/psyc372/pdf/4-8-memory-stuctures.pdf

[60] Pendick, D. Harvard Health Publications. (2016) "7 common causes of forgetfulness" Retrieved from http://www.health.harvard.edu/blog/7-common-causes-of-forgetfulness-201302225923

[61] American Psychological Association. (n.d.) "Trauma" Retrieved from https://www.apa.org/topics/trauma

[62] New South Wales Law Foundation. (2006) *On the edge of justice: the legal needs of people with mental illness* Retrieved from www.lawfoundation.net.au/ljf/app/694983f6c81d1910ca25718e00057f4e.html

[63] WebMD Medical Reference. (2016) "Causes of Mental Illness" Retrieved from http://www.webmd.com/mental-health/mental-health-causes-mental-illness#2

[64] CTV News Network. (2016) "Healthcare wait times hit 20 weeks in 2016" Retrieved from http://www.ctvnews.ca/health/healthcare-wait-times-hit-20-weeks-in-2016-report-1.3171718

[65] Emery, J.E., Feasby, T.E., Forster, A.J., Magnan, S., Shojania, K.G., Tubman, M. The United States National Center for Biotechnology Information. (2009) *Management of MRI Lists in Canada.* Retrieved from https://www.ncbi.nlm.nih.gov/pmc/articles/PMC2653696/

[66] Mayo Clinic. (2016) "Compulsive Gambling" Retrieved from http://www.mayoclinic.org/diseases-conditions/compulsive-gambling/home/ovc-20258391
Psychology Today. (2017) "Gambling Disorder (Compulsive Gambling, Pathological Gambling)" Retrieved from https://www.psychologytoday.com/conditions/gambling-disorder-compulsive-gambling-pathological-gambling

[67] Stein, J. The Washington Post. (2018) "U.S. Military Budget inches closer to $1 trillion mark, as concerns over federal deficit grow." Retrieved from https://www.washingtonpost.com/news/wonk/wp/2018/06/19/u-s-military-budget-inches-closer-to-1-trillion-mark-as-concerns-over-federal-deficit-grow/
NR staff writer. National Review. (2018) "Total Welfare Spending now at $1 Trillion" Retrieved

from https://www.nationalreview.com/corner/
total-welfare-spending-now-1-trillion-nro-staff/
   Clemons, S. The Atlantic (2012) "The Real Defense Budget"
Retrieved from https://www.theatlantic.com/politics/
archive/2012/02/the-real-defense-budget/253327/

[68] The Salvation Army. (n.d.) "Why are people homeless?" Retrieved
from http://www.salvationarmy.org.au/en/Who-We-Are/
our-work/Homelessness/Why-are-people-homeless/

[69] Davidson, J.D. The Federalist (2019) "The Entire
News Media is Biased. They should just embrace it."
Retrieved from https://thefederalist.com/2019/09/19/
the-entire-news-media-is-biased-they-should-just-embrace-it/
   Hallin, D. Center For Media Literacy (n.d.) "Whatever
Happened to the News?" Retrieved from https://www.medialit.
org/reading-room/whatever-happened-news

[70] Quran su 3 vs 2 - 3, su 29 vs 46
   Deutsche Welle. (2015) "Why 'Islamic State' is terrorizing
Christians" Retrieved from http://www.dw.com/en/
why-islamic-state-is-terrorizing-christians/a-18286141
   Raghavan, S. The Washington Post (2014) "Tens of thousands
of Muslims flee Christian Militia in Central African Republic"
Retrieved from https://www.washingtonpost.com/world/africa/
tens-of-thousands-of-muslims-flee-christian-militias-in-central-
african-republic/2014/02/07/5a1adbb2-9032-11e3-84e1-27626c5ef5fb_
story.html

[71] the buddhist centre. (n.d.) "What is Buddhism?" Retrieved from
https://thebuddhistcentre.com/buddhism

[72] Carlson, R. The Balance Small Business (2019) "Conglomerate and
Congeneric" Retrieved from https://www.thebalancesmb.com/
conglomerate-and-cogeneric-mergers-392843
   Hargrave, M. Investopedia (2019) "Merger" Retrieved from
https://www.investopedia.com/terms/m/merger.asp

[73] Walling, W.E. JSTOR The Annals of the American Academy
of Political and Social Science, Vol. 26, Federal Regulation

of Corporations, pp. 109-127 (1905) "British and American Trade Unionism" Retrieved from https://www.jstor.org/stable/1010586?seq=1

[74] The Federal Reserve Bank of San Francisco. (2002) *What are some of the factors that contribute to a rise in inflation?* Retrieved from http://www.frbsf.org/education/publications/doctor-econ/2002/october/inflation-factors-rise/

[75] Morah, C. Investopedia. (n.d.) "What causes a recession?" Retrieved from http://www.investopedia.com/ask/answers/08/cause-of-recession.asp

[76] Amadeo, K. The Balance. (2017) "What Caused the 2008 Global Financial Crisis?" Retrieved from https://www.thebalance.com/what-caused-2008-global-financial-crisis-3306176
Positive Money. (n.d.) "Financial Crisis & Recessions" Retrieved from http://positivemoney.org/issues/recessions-crisis/

[77] Washington Reuters (2013) "Fed missed warning signs in 2007 as crisis gathered steam" Retrieved from https://www.theglobeandmail.com/report-on-business/economy/us-fed-missed-warning-signs-in-2007-as-crisis-gathered-steam/article7526832/

[78] Chen, J. Investopedia (2020) "Stock Market" Retrieved from https://www.investopedia.com/terms/s/stockmarket.asp
Hayes, A. Investopedia (2020) "Bond" Retrieved from https://www.investopedia.com/terms/b/bond.asp
Hall, M. Investopedia (2019) "Options vs Futures: What's the difference?" Retrieved from https://www.investopedia.com/ask/answers/difference-between-options-and-futures/
Newall, P., Weiss-Cohen, L. NIH Public Library of Medicine. "The Gamblification of Investing: How a New Generation of Investors Is Being Born to Lose" (2022) Retrieved from https://www.ncbi.nlm.nih.gov/pmc/articles/PMC9105963/
The Globe and Mail. (n.d.) "Learning curve for futures trading is steep" Retrieved from http://www.theglobeandmail.com/globe-investor/investment-ideas/learning-curve-for-futures-trading-is-steep/article4201259/

[79] Science Daily. (n.d.) "Workaholic" Retrieved from https://www.sciencedaily.com/terms/workaholic.htm

[80] Population Institute Canada. (n.d.) "Overpopulation - a growing threat to global food security" Retrieved from https://populationinstitutecanada.ca/overpopulation-a-growing-threat-to-global-food-security/
DW. (n.d.) "Sustainable food for everyone? The challenge of our century" Retrieved from https://www.dw.com/en/environment-world-population-day-agriculture-sustainability-food-waste-food-security-overpopulation/a-39628974

[81] The Physics Factbook. *Area of Earth's Land Surface* Science Desk Reference American Scientific: Wiley, 1999: 180. Retrieved from https://hypertextbook.com/facts/2001/DanielChen.shtml
Arctic Guide. (2017) "What is the Size of Antarctica" Retrieved from http://antarcticguide.com/about-antarctica/antarctic-geography/how-big-is-antarctica/

[82] Reddit Ask Science. (2013) "How much land does it take to support one human being?" Retrieved from https://www.reddit.com/r/askscience/comments/1aozn1/how_much_land_does_it_take_to_support_one_human/

[83] Costello, C. et al. Nature (2020) *The Future of Food from the Sea* Retrieved from https://www.nature.com/articles/s41586-020-2616-y#:~:text=Food%20from%20the%20sea%20is,Supplementary%20Tables%201%E2%80%933).

[84] Manhattan Engineer District of the United States. (1946) *The Atomic Bombings of Hiroshima and Nagasaki* Retrieved from http://www.abomb1.org/hiroshim/hiro_med.html

[85] Berkeley Education. (n.d.) *Science aims to explain and understand* Retrieved from https://undsci.berkeley.edu/article/0_0_0/whatisscience_04

[86] Chavez, H. Lifehack (n.d.) "10 Ways Technology Can Make Your Life Easier And More Secure" Retrieved from https://www.lifehack.org/451123/10-ways-technology-can-make-your-life-easier-and-more-secure

[87]   Howell, E. Live Science. (2017) "Unified Field Theory: Tying It All Together" Retrieved from https://www.livescience.com/58861-unified-field-theory.html

Strassler, M. Of Particular Significance: Conversations about science with theoretical physicist Matt Strassler. (2013, February 25) "What Holds Nuclei Together?" Retrieved from https://profmattstrassler.com/articles-and-posts/particle-physics-basics/the-structure-of-matter/the-nuclei-of-atoms-at-the-heart-of-matter/what-holds-nuclei-together/

Lucas, J. Live Science (2014) "What is the Weak Force?" Retrieved from https://www.livescience.com/49254-weak-force.html

[88]   Mann, A. Live Science. "What is Quantum Mechanics" (2022) Retrieved from https://www.livescience.com/33816-quantum-mechanics-explanation.html

[89]   Tate, K. Live Science. (2013) "How Quantum Entanglement Works" Retrieved from http://www.livescience.com/28550-how-quantum-entanglement-works-infographic.html

[90]   Dictionary.com. (n.d.) "Quantum Bit" Retrieved from http://www.dictionary.com/browse/qubit

[91]   TechTarget. (n.d.) "Quantum Computing" Retrieved from http://whatis.techtarget.com/definition/quantum-computing

[92]   Quantum Computing Report (n.d.) "The Best Applications for Quantum Computing" Retrieved from https://quantumcomputingreport.com/our-take/the-best-applications-for-quantum-computing/

Vella, M. Time.com. (2014) "9 Ways Quantum Computing Will Change Everything" Retrieved from http://time.com/5035/9-ways-quantum-computing-will-change-everything/

[93]   Malik, S., Muhammad, K., Waheed, Y. NIH National Library of Medicine. "Nanotechnology: A Revolution in Modern Industry" (2023) Retrieved from https://www.ncbi.nlm.nih.gov/pmc/articles/PMC9865684/

[94] Understandingnano.com. (2007) "Nanotechnology Applications: A Variety of Uses" Retrieved from http://www.understandingnano.com/nanotech-applications.html

[95] Government of Canada: Department of Justice (2017) "Criminal and Civil Cases - About Canada's System of Justice" Retrieved from https://www.justice.gc.ca/eng/csj-sjc/just/08.html
Duigan, B. Encyclopaedia Britannica. (n.d.) "What is the difference between Criminal and Civil Law?" Retrieved from https://www.britannica.com/story/what-is-the-difference-between-criminal-law-and-civil-law

[96] Government of Canada, Department of Justice. (n.d.) "How does Canada's Court System Work?" Retrieved from https://www.justice.gc.ca/eng/csj-sjc/ccs-ajc/01.html
American Bar Association. (2019) "How Courts Work" Retrieved from https://www.americanbar.org/groups/public_education/resources/law_related_education_network/how_courts_work/cases/

[97] Cliff Notes. (2016) "The Nature of Police Work" Retrieved from https://www.cliffsnotes.com/study-guides/criminal-justice/police-function/the-nature-of-police-work

[98] Legal Match. "What Does a Civil Litigation Lawyer Do?" (n.d.) Retrieved from https://www.legalmatch.com/law-library/article/civil-law-and-civil-attorneys.html

[99] Pearlman, J. The Telegraph. (2016) "1 in 5 CEOs are psychopaths, study finds" Retrieved from http://www.telegraph.co.uk/news/2016/09/13/1-in-5-ceos-are-psychopaths-australian-study-finds/

[100] Rose-Innes, O. Healt24. (2015) "How to recognize a Psychopath" Retrieved from http://www.health24.com/Mental-Health/Disorders/How-to-recognise-a-psychopath-20120721

[101] NKJV Bible. Genesis ch 1 vs 27

[102] Sdorf, C.F. The Atlantic. (2016) "Do Humans Inherit or Create Their Personalities?" Retrieved from

https://www.theatlantic.com/health/archive/2016/06/
do-humans-inherit-or-create-their-personalities/489266/

[103] Hiskey, D. Today I Found Out (2019) "Why is the Stereotypical
Image of Aliens Green/Grey Bald Humanoids?" Retrieved from
https://www.todayifoundout.com/index.php/2019/09/why-
is-the-stereotypical-image-of-aliens-green-grey-bald-
humanoids/#google_vignette
    Paranormal-Encyclopedia.com (n.d.) "Aliens in Popular
Culture" Retrieved from http://www.paranormal-encyclopedia.
com/a/alien/popular-culture/

[104] Careless, J. Asphalt: The Magazine of the Asphalt Institute. (2017)
"Reducing road noise with pavement design" Retrieved from
http://asphaltmagazine.com/turning-the-volume-down/

[105] Franco, F. Ph.D. PsychCentral (2020) "How Intergenerational
Trauma Impacts Families" Retrieved from https://psychcentral.
com/lib/how-intergenerational-trauma-impacts-families#1
    Domoney, J., Trevillion, K. Infant Mental Health Journal (2020)
*A qualitative interview study of men participating in a perinatal
program to reduce violence.* Retreived from https://onlinelibrary.
wiley.com/doi/full/10.1002/imhj.21886
    Jaffee, S.R. Ph.D., et al. US National Library of Medicine
National Institutes of Health (2013) *Safe, Stable, Nurturing
Relationships Break the Intergenerational Cycle of Abuse:
A Prospective Nationally Representative Cohort of Children in the
United Kingdom* Retrieved from https://www.ncbi.nlm.nih.gov/
pmc/articles/PMC4212819/

[106] Bible Info. (n.d.) "What is Heaven like and where is Heaven?"
Retrieved from https://www.bibleinfo.com/en/questions/
where-is-heaven

[107] Bulletin of Atomic Scientists. (2017) "Doomsday Clock" Retrieved
from https://thebulletin.org/doomsday-clock/

[108] Maranville, C. Life, Hope, & Truth (n.d.) "What Does It Mean To
Be Saved?" Retrieved from https://lifehopeandtruth.com/change/
salvation/what-does-it-mean-to-be-saved/

[109] WhitBourne, S.K. Psychology Today. (2015) "What happens when a psychopath falls in love" Retrieved from https://www.psychologytoday.com/blog/fulfillment-any-age/201505/what-happens-when-psychopath-falls-in-love

[110] Hedge, C. The New York Times. (2003) "What Every Person Should Know About War" Retrieved from https://www.nytimes.com/2003/07/06/books/chapters/what-every-person-should-know-about-war.html

[111] Encyclopaedia Britannica (n.d.) "Mutual Assured Destruction" Retrieved from https://www.britannica.com/topic/mutual-assured-destruction

[112] Summers, L. Financial Times. (2017) "Trump's Alarming G20 Performance" Retrieved from https://www.ft.com/content/ea2849ea-6335-11e7-8814-0ac7eb84e5f1
Daily Kos (2017) Der Spiegel: "It's Time to Get Rid of Donald Trump" (Updated) Retrieved from https://www.dailykos.com/stories/2017/5/25/1666167/-Der-Spiegel-It-s-Time-to-Get-Rid-of-Donald-Trump
Lee, B. The Guardian. (2018) "Trump is now dangerous - that makes his mental health a matter of public interest" Retrieved from theguardian.com/commentisfree/2018/jan/07/donald-trump-dangerous-psychiatrist

[113] Calamur, K. The Atlantic. (2017) "North Korea Keeps Up Its Provocations" Retrieved from https://www.theatlantic.com/international/archive/2017/09/north-korea-missile-test/539121/
Bender, B. Politico. (2022) "How the Ukraine war could go nuclear" Retrieved from https://www.politico.com/news/2022/03/24/how-ukraine-war-could-go-nuclear-00019899

[114] WIL Bible CEV Revelation ch 5 vs 5-6

[115] Davenport, B. Live Bold & Bloom. (2017) "20 Good Character Traits Essential for Happiness" Retrieved from https://liveboldandbloom.com/10/relationships/good-character-traits

[116] English Standard Version Bible. Revelation ch 3 vs10